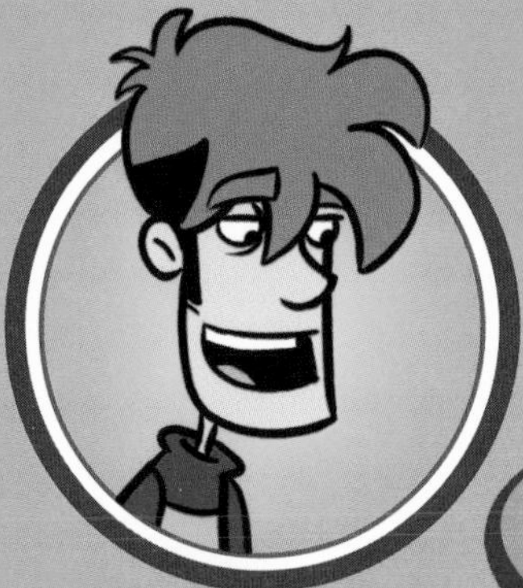

PENNY ARCADE 7

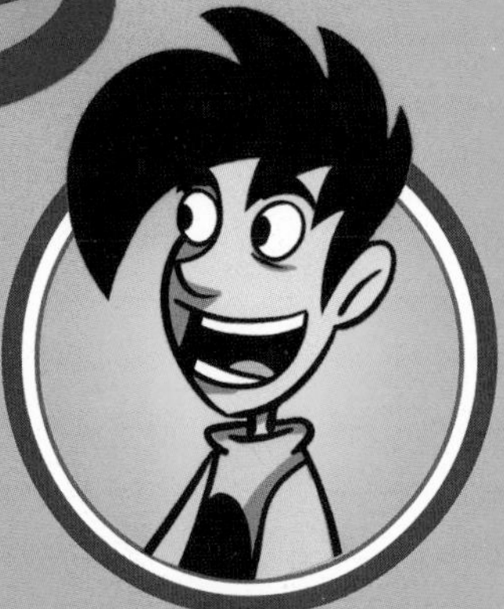

PENNY ARCADE 1

  **BALLANTINE BOOKS • NEW YORK**

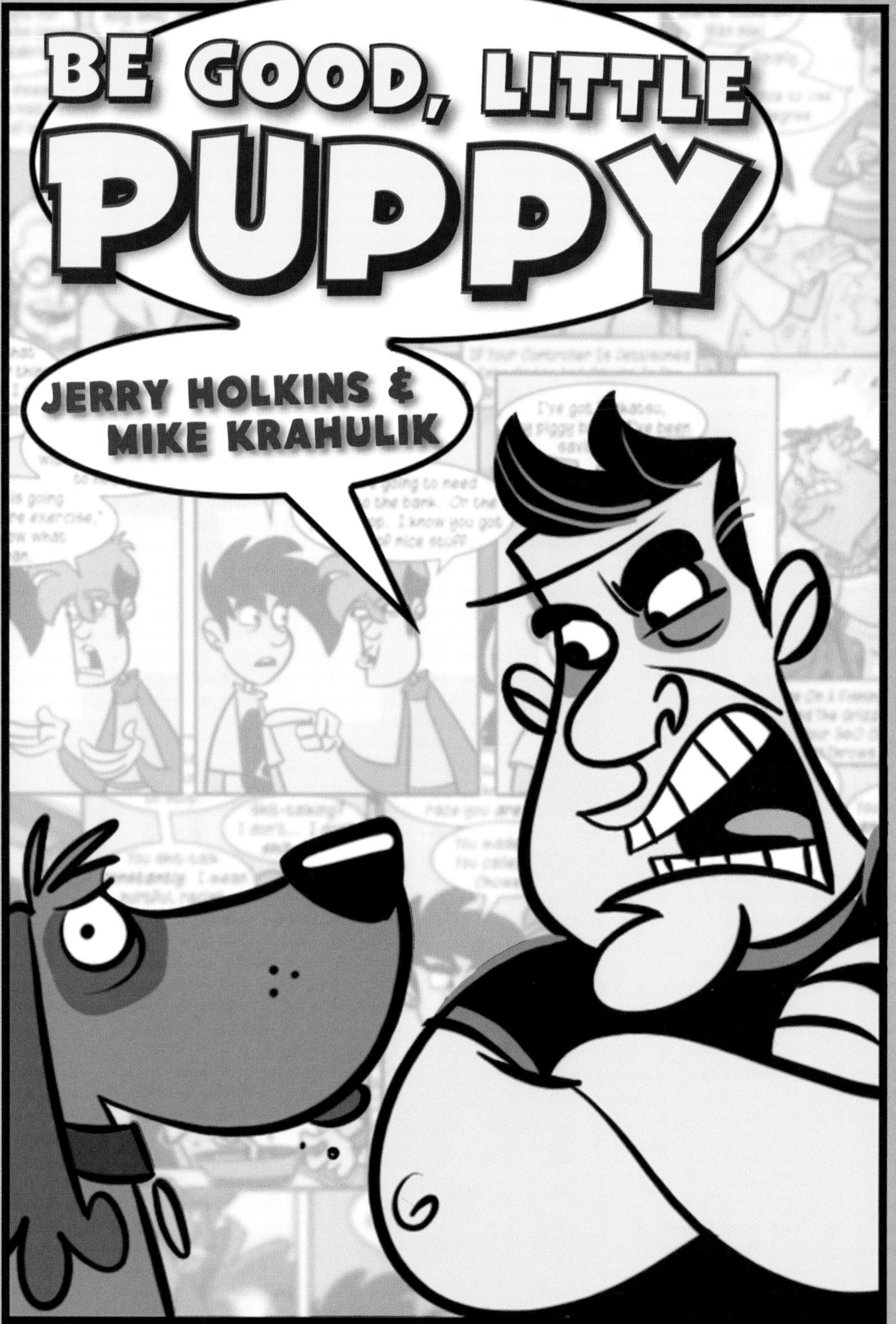
BE GOOD, LITTLE PUPPY
JERRY HOLKINS & MIKE KRAHULIK

Published in the United States by Del Rey, an imprint of The Random House Publishing Group, a division of Random House, Inc., New York.

Del Rey is a registered trademark and the Del Rey colophon is a trademark of Random House, Inc.

Penny Arcade copyright © 1998 Penny Arcade, Inc. PENNY ARCADE and all related characters and the distinctive likenesses thereof: ™ and © 1998, Penny Arcade, Inc. Licensed by Penny Arcade, Inc. All rights reserved.

ISBN 978-0-345-51228-4

Printed in the United States of America

www.delreybooks.com
www.penny-arcade.com

9 8 7 6 5 4 3 2 1

Book design by Simon M. Sullivan

FOREWORD

When the guys at *Penny Arcade* asked me to write an intro to their next book, I was flattered. Not only am I a huge fan, but I'd just finished writing a four-hundred-thousand-word novel. Writing a little intro for a comic I love would be like a vacation. How long should it be? Two thousand words? Ha. I laugh at two thousand words.

But now, as I sit down to actually write it, I realize I don't have the first clue as to what I'm doing here. I don't read introductions, as a rule. I certainly don't write them. I don't have the slightest idea what I'm supposed to write here.

I'm probably supposed to explain to you why *Penny Arcade* is awesome. But if you're holding this book, odds are you're already a fan. You know that *Penny Arcade* is the pinnacle of cool geekery. You know when Mike and Jerry combine their powers they form a vast four-armed, four-legged being that strides the Internet like some colossal pre-hubris Greek. You know this already. There's no point in me telling you shit you already know . . .

So, looking for inspiration, I started to read some of the *Penny Arcade* archive. Then I decided if I was going to read the archive, I should probably start at the beginning . . .

As a result, I can now tell you something you don't already know. If you read the *Penny Arcade* archives from the beginning to the end, it will take you about seven and a half hours. You will hurt with laughter.

Also, your girlfriend will get upset with you for ignoring her for pretty much an entire day.

But even after reading all the strips from beginning to end, I still don't know what I'm supposed to write. So, lacking any better ideas, I guess I'll tell you a story. Because that's what I do.

Ready? Here we go.

A couple of months ago, I meet up with some friends I haven't seen since college. We grab dinner, trade gaming stories, then catch up on one another's lives a bit. These are the folks who knew me back when I was, for lack of a better term, a pathetic slacker.

I'm not being humble here. I took nine years to get my undergrad degree. I was the guy who worked on his mammoth, unpublished fantasy novel for over twelve years. If anything, slacker is rather generous.

These days things are different. My first book was a ridiculous success, and my friends want to know the details. What's it like finally being published? What's it like, winning awards, being invited to conventions, getting fan mail from all over the world?

They're excited for me. They want to hear that my life is distilled awesome, that my days are sybaritic orgies filled with adoring catgirls and cherry-flavored Pez.

But these are my friends, so I tell them the truth. "Some of it is okay," I say. "Fan mail is nice, but it takes a lot of time to answer it all. Conventions are fun, I like hanging out with fans. But it's exhausting, too."

My friends look like they don't quite believe me. Still, they say, it's cool, isn't it? You hit the *New York Times* bestseller list with your first book. That was awesome, right?

I shrug. "I remember getting the call from my agent. He was pretty excited." I look over at my girlfriend. "Did we do anything to celebrate that?"

"We ordered Chinese food," she says, "and watched *Dr. Who.*"

My friends look at me, and I can tell they're confused. Don't I understand that I am Living the Dream? Why aren't I bubbling with joy?

"It's mostly stressful," I tell them. "Deadlines. Revisions. I should feel like a rock star. But I don't. Sometimes I wonder if the last couple of years burned out a fuse in my brain. I don't seem to be enjoying all of this as much as I should." I shrug.

There's a moment of uncomfortable silence at the table.

"You were pretty excited when the guys from *Penny Arcade* called," my girlfriend points out.

This makes me smile. It's not a little smile, either. It's a big shit-eating grin. It's the smile I wore all the time when I was back in college. "That was cool," I say.

That's when I realize the truth. The one thing I've really enjoyed these last couple of years is getting to meet cool people. Felicia Day showed up at one of my book signings. I got to have lunch with Peter S. Beagle. I rode the world's largest carousel at House on the Rock with Neil Gaiman.

And, after a long campaign of quietly, carefully stalking them, I've finally gotten to know the guys who create *Penny Arcade.* When I first found out they'd called and left a message for me, I was giddy as a schoolgirl. A great big beardy schoolgirl.

More than that. I was nervous. When I got their message, I had to go for a little walk to calm myself down. Even then, as I dialed the number to call them back, my palms were sweaty.

It's not just that Mike and Jerry are such a brilliant creative team. It's not just that *Penny Arcade* has become one of the monolithic pillars of geek society.

It's not even the fact that they consistently bring the funny. Not just a little funny, either. Over the years, *Penny Arcade* has been a reliable source of laugh-out-loud humor. The sort of funny where I end up over at a friend's house asking, "Have you read today's PA?"

Any of those would be good reasons for me to have sweaty palms. But the real reason is this: I've been reading *Penny Arcade* since the very beginning. I started in 1999, and while other comics have come and gone, *Penny Arcade* has always been there. For more than a decade, it's been like the soundtrack for my life.

I remember reading them early on when I was still in college. I remember their rivalry with *User Friendly.* I read hundreds if not thousands of The Bench strips. (Whatever happened to that, by the way?) It's because of *Penny Arcade* that I played System Shock 2.

Later, when I moved across the country to go to grad school, *Penny Arcade* helped keep me sane. I had to keep my head down, be respectable, and choke down my bile-laden rage at the stupidity of academia. But *Penny Arcade* was there for me, venting bile enough for both of us. Other times, they gave me a laugh when I really, really needed a laugh.

But there's more to *Penny Arcade* than dick jokes and frothy rage. Over the years, they've shown that they're also consummate storytellers. I remember exactly where I was sitting back in

2002 when I read Jerry's post about eating carrot cake and thought, This guy can really write. Mike never ceases to amaze me when he tries on a different style of art.

I bought the ill-fated first book. I played the game. I bought the T-shirt. I was there when they tapped a previously undiscovered Jungian archetype with the cardboard tube. In 2005 I used their letter to Jack Thompson to teach my students the definition of satire.

I was one of the first people to donate to Child's Play, and I watched with delight while it spiraled into madness. Years later, when I had my own fans, I started my own charity. I don't know if I would have had the guts to do that if I hadn't seen *Penny Arcade* try it first.

The book you're holding contains all of *Penny Arcade* from 2006, a year that holds some of my favorite strips, including "I Hope You Like Text." I'll resist the urge to talk more about them here since you'll be reading them soon enough.

The year 2006 was a big one for me. It was the year I finally sold my novel. It was also the year I started officially stalking *Penny Arcade.* You see, I wanted nothing more than for them to read my book.

I knew it was dangerous. They do not pull punches. If they think something is shit, they say so in no uncertain terms. Still, I'd been reading their stuff for years and loving it. I hoped beyond hope that they might like my book, if only I could get them to try it.

For years I plotted and maneuvered. I sent copies of my book to their office. I had my loyal minions give them copies at conventions. I went to San Diego Comic-Con, but was too bashful to approach them, and instead merely gazed on them lovingly from afar.

Then, in 2010, Jerry called my house. Sweaty-palmed and anxious, I returned his call. I honestly can't remember what I said, but I'm guessing it wasn't very coherent.

There's only one part of the conversation I recall clearly. Jerry told me that he liked my book. I responded by gushing about how much I love the comic.

"Cool," Jerry said, "let's be best friends."

It gave me a big warm fuzzy. I remember thinking, Can we do that? Is it that easy?

Later that year, I worked up the courage to introduce myself at Comic-Con. Jerry was nice enough to read the beta-test version of my second novel and give me feedback. Mike liked the first book enough that he stole parts for his D&D campaign. That's the sincerest form of flattery as far as I'm concerned.

So, without any further rambling on my part, I'd like to introduce you to two of my best friends. They do a little webcomic called *Penny Arcade.*

It's pretty good. I think you might like it.

• • •

PATRICK ROTHFUSS,
NEW YORK TIMES BESTSELLING AUTHOR OF *THE NAME OF THE WIND* AND *THE WISE MAN'S FEAR*
FEBRUARY 14, 2011

INTRODUCTION

With twelve full years of unparalleled creation under my belt, and the seventh compilation here in your hands, there can be no doubt: I have taken the yoke of the Earth and bent it to my purpose. The time has come for me to burst free from this earthly body, to sail the Amethyst waves of the Aetherion.

I cannot know what form I will take. I cannot know if my consciousness will spread like spores, to burrow into the meat of the human mind, to dwell inside a thought-house. I might also be myself, or something like myself, except one of my arms will be a lobster. Not a lobster arm, mind you, or like a claw, but an entire lobster just fuckin' right there that's all like "What's up." That's a lot to take in, for me *and* the lobster, and I hope that we can overcome our differences and that he is able to breathe oxygen somehow.

It's happening! I can feel myself leaving I can feeeeeeeeeeeeeee

You know what, I just came back to my body from the Amethyst of the Aetherion or whatever, and it was pretty dumb. It was just like being at Taco Bell, except everything was sort of purple. It was like being at a purple Taco Bell.

• • •

TYCHO BRAHE
SEATTLE, WASHINGTON

WEALTH BEYOND MEASURE

January 2, 2006 · There were a rash of these, as you might recall: eBay "auctions" where the thing being offered was actually a photograph of something you might want. It was a profound step forward for the service, because *previously* when you were trying to screw someone, you sent them nothing. Shipping something that exists must be seen as an infinite improvement.

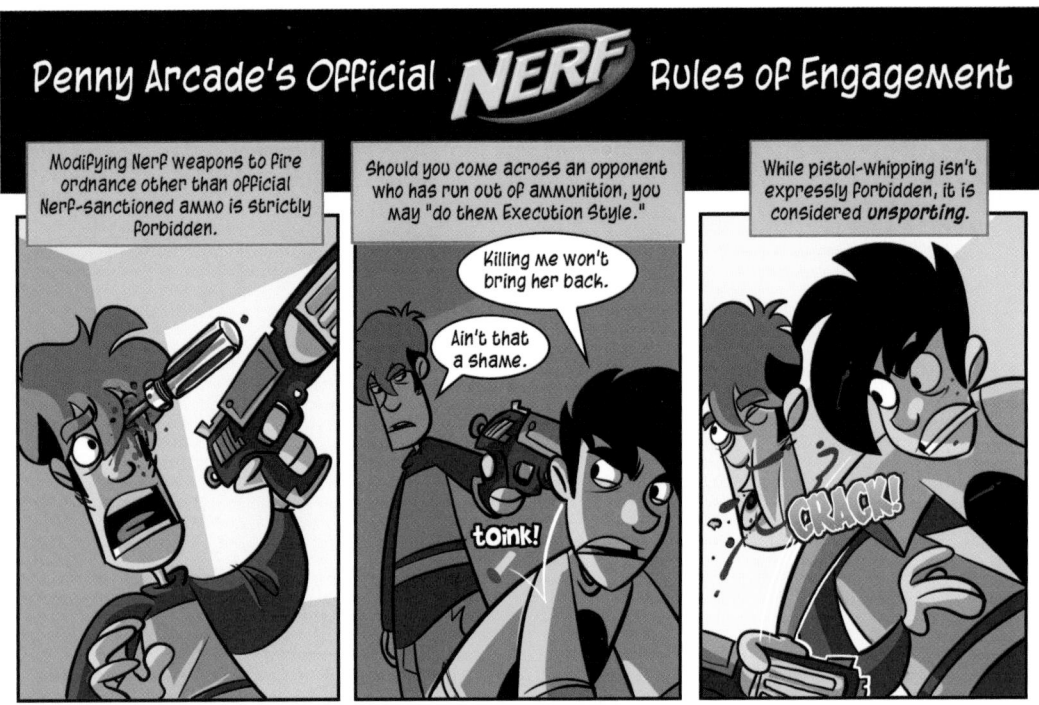

REALLY MORE OF A LOOSE GUIDELINE

January 4, 2006 · The Nerf Phase was fairly pronounced, fueled (as it was) by a move into a larger office space that could house such conflicts. It was during this time that Gabriel invented the "Scorpion Round," which differed from a normal round in that the rubberized tip was replaced by a pushpin. The Nerf Phase ended shortly thereafter.

BOTTOM TOPPINGS

January 6, 2006 · As I suggested, we've just celebrated the twelfth anniversary of *Penny Arcade* as a full-production jpeg foundry, and it's kind of a wonder to me, because there are very, very few things Gabriel and I can agree on. Ordering a simple pizza is an almost apocalyptic affair, rife with seething and recriminations and always very nearly on the ragged edge of murder.

BFF!

January 9, 2006 · It's rarely discussed these days, especially since the old Live network was shut down, but the ability of the Xbox 360 to play games from the legacy box was once a thing to discuss. The list of games would expand from time to time as they tooled around with the emulation, but there were always a few games that never quite squared with the imagined demographics.

OH MY DEAR SWEET LORD

January 11, 2006 · The advent of Intel processors cropping up in Apple computers eroded the last few nanometers of my pro-PC patina. I'm on my second Mac now, another iMac, which for work purposes is more than enough. "Work" for me is just typing words, though, so technically I could probably get by without much more than a nice calculator.

DNDA

January 13, 2006 · It really didn't have dragons, then. It traveled a very strange road, for a very long time, until developer Turbine Entertainment placed a bet on free-to-play that increased revenues by 500 percent. It wasn't really what I think of as "D&D," but it wasn't beholden to overgrown genre tropes and received wisdom, either. Bold, in its way.

JESUS IS MY GUILD LEADER

January 16, 2006 · In that day's post, I wonder aloud why you don't see more games with explicitly Christian themes. There was that RTS based on Left Behind as I recall, but that's more a game *for* Christians than it is a game *about* Christ. I stopped attending church when I was eighteen, and stopped believing the things they said there even before that, but I never stopped loving the Bible.

SAVANNAH HEAT

January 18, 2006 · Gabe and Tycho are not unlike ourselves, but I couldn't tell you exactly where this thing with the animals started. It's true that I do like to look at the entire Internet—there's a lot of stuff on it, and I like to challenge my assumptions about any number of things. Sensual giraffes don't really figure in. Indeed, a giraffe in a bikini might be a nice change of pace.

5

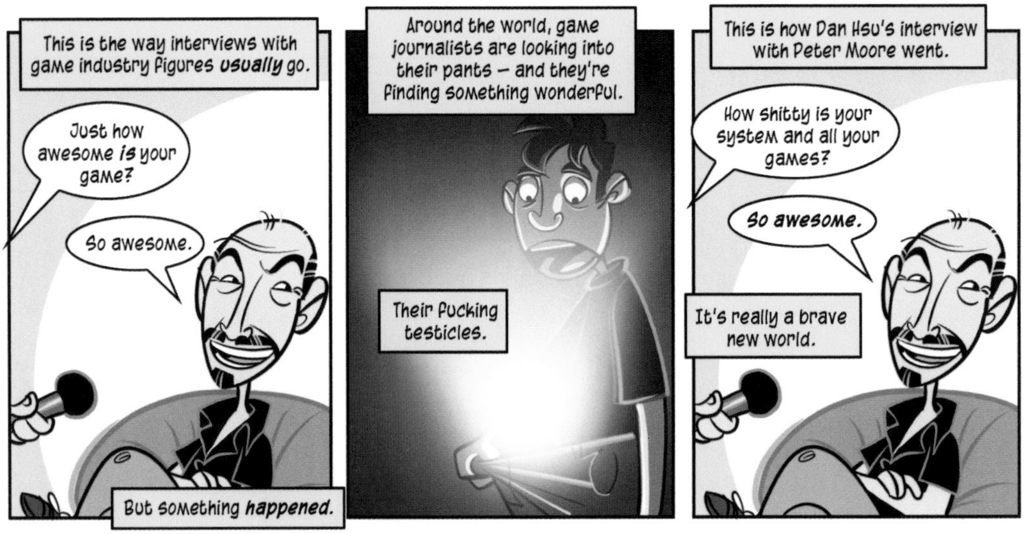
This is the way interviews with game industry figures *usually* go.
Just how awesome *is* your game?
So awesome.
But something *happened.*
Around the world, game journalists are looking into their pants – and they're finding something wonderful.
Their fucking testicles.
This is how Dan Hsu's interview with Peter Moore went.
How shitty is your system and all your games?
So awesome.
It's really a brave new world.

THE PARTIAL REVOLUTION

January 20, 2006 · I was curious at the time if this was going to spark a trend of some kind, this BBC-School-For-Brutal-Interrogators-type stuff, but it didn't really. There's certainly plenty of writing counter to the message of a Microsoft or a Sony, but it's largely content-free snark, and raw press releases get snapped up before and after, so what difference does it make?

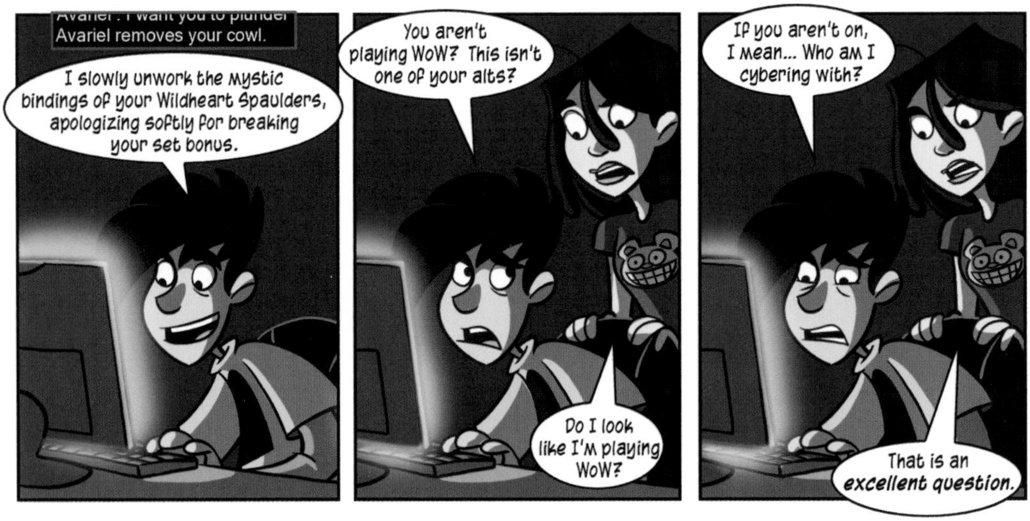
Avariel removes your cowl.
I slowly unwork the mystic bindings of your Wildheart Spaulders, apologizing softly for breaking your set bonus.
You aren't playing WoW? This isn't one of your alts?
Do I look like I'm playing WoW?
If you aren't on, I mean... Who am I cybering with?
That is an *excellent question.*

ELDRITCH EROTICA

January 23, 2006 · This is a thing that actually happened, which was great, because we have to write comics sometimes and it helps if something terrible happens at home.

Write your own Preview

1/22/06

AN EA GAMES MASTERPIECE!

Black is probably the most stunning EA game ever. The visuals are so stunning for the Xbox. Although I love playing online, Black should definitely be focused on an intense single player experience. Black is exactly what I've been looking for. Black #1 shooter of the year for Xbox.

ON BOTANY

January 25, 2006 · The post at the top of the comic is real, though it may be hard to believe. Once you become aware of the fact that PR companies regularly pose as human beings in places where gaming enthusiasts are likely to gather, it gives true paranoia a chance to take root. Then again, people are perfectly capable of saying dumb shit without being explicitly on the payroll. I'm of the ironclad opinion that most message boards are just PerlScripts talking to themselves and one another, over and over and over.

A FIELD WITH VIRTUALLY UNLIMITED POTENTIAL

January 27, 2006 · I remember the vast majority of my strip-writing processes, and there are sometimes things encoded in the dialogue or the art that communicate on a peculiar band. But I'll be Goddamned if there's anything, *anywhere* in this strip that can tell me why there is a pig here, what we're doing there, or why in God's name the creature needs to be waxed so bad.

GOOD MONEY AFTER ALMOST INCALCULABLY BAD

January 30, 2006 · What's kind of funny about Infinium Labs and the whole Phantom thing is that now, in 2011, a dedicated gaming PC with access to digital downloads doesn't seem all that weird. Every person who plays games on a computer more or less has that kind of setup already. At the time, though, it seemed pretty much like Crazytown.

MR. (PENETRAT)ED

February 1, 2006 · I don't know if this story is true, and I haven't made much of an effort to find out. This is something that I'm perfectly okay not knowing.

COST CUTTING MEASURES

February 3, 2006 · Robert Khoo, who operates the business side of the sprawling *Penny Arcade* Empire, often suggests that the company can reap incredible savings simply by getting rid of us. I came at it a different way: What if we only got rid of Gabriel? That way we can mitigate those Gabriel-related costs, and, um . . . I will still have a job.

IN THE HOUSE OF BOGGS

February 6, 2006 ·
At the annual Child's Play Charity Dinner and Auction, a hotly contested item year after year is an appearance in the strip. It cracked twenty-five thousand dollars one year, which I think we can all agree is a big ol' pile of dollars. In 2006, Christian Boggs took the prize for a mere twenty thou, which I guess is less. But it's still a lot.

And that shit be intimidating.

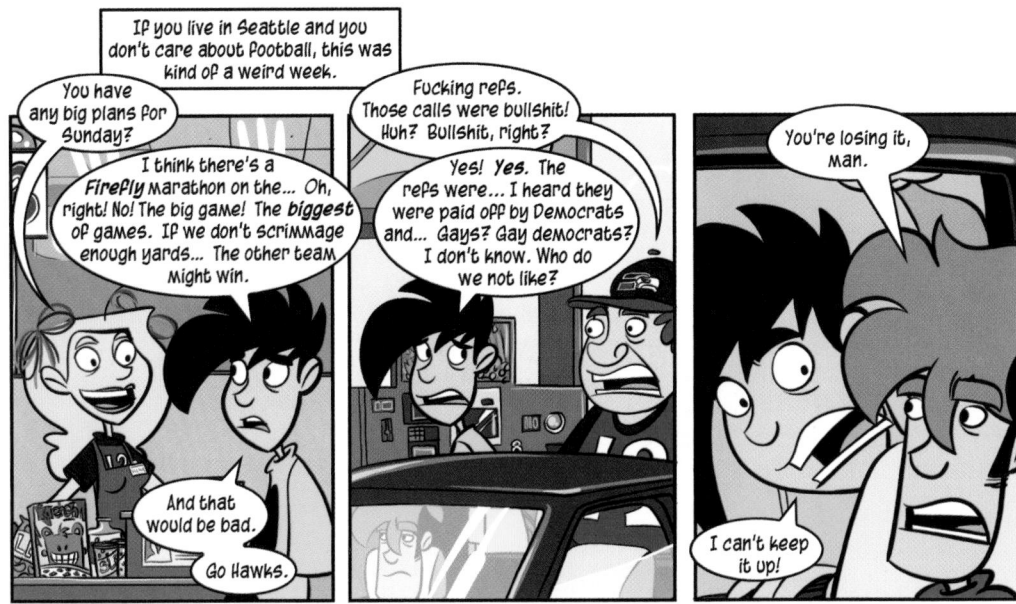

THE SPORTING LIFE

February 8, 2006 · I said in the post for this strip that I was done with games where I had no say in the outcome, and I've stuck to it. Watching "my" team get eviscerated during this Super Bowl (which is apparently the best of all the bowls) was exhausting, both physically and emotionally. I'm glad that following the rise and fall of a sports team was never in my DNA. I'd be a fucking basket case. I didn't handle it well at all.

THEY ARE AMONG US

February 10, 2006 · After we did that earlier strip about "plants" on forums, we were drowned in a vast reservoir of information from insiders about the true extent of the practice. What we learned is that it's *practiced extensively.* Recall that later in 2006, Sony (through a campaign by Zipatoni) operated a fake PSP fan site for the holidays. When people think about what they want for Christmas, the answer is very rarely lies.

PRECISION ORDNANCE

February 13, 2006 · To the extent that one can be a fan of one's own work and get away with it, it makes me happy whenever Annarchy (aka Anne-Claire Forthwith) shows up in one of these compilations. Every panel bows and molds itself to accommodate her. Everything in her immediate vicinity is improved.

FOR THE LOVE OF GOD PLEASE PLAY OUR GAME

February 15, 2006 · It's fun to be a jerk or whatever, and sometimes my job requires it. The thing is, what they chose to do here—that is to say, get the client in the hands of players—is today considered the sensible model for this kind of thing. Server consolidation, free-to-play, all the old hallmarks of MMO Apocalypse are business as usual these days.

LIES AND MORE LIES

February 17, 2006 · This arrangement was far more common when we still lived together, in an apartment (specifically, Apartment 26) on Spokane's North Side. At least, it was the North Side when we were still living there. I just got back, and the town just keeps migrating ever more northward, until what had been north is now somewhere around the middle.

IN WHICH FAIR FOOD MAKES AN APPEARANCE

February 20, 2006 · I sometimes try to explain to my son that there is such a place, one that will fry a Twinkie, and he assumes that I'm just fucking around with him—that bliss at this raw threshold isn't available terrestrially, that it can only be *earned* as the result of a good life and divine grace. It's like that when I try to describe any carnival food—elephant ears, funnel cakes, all of it.

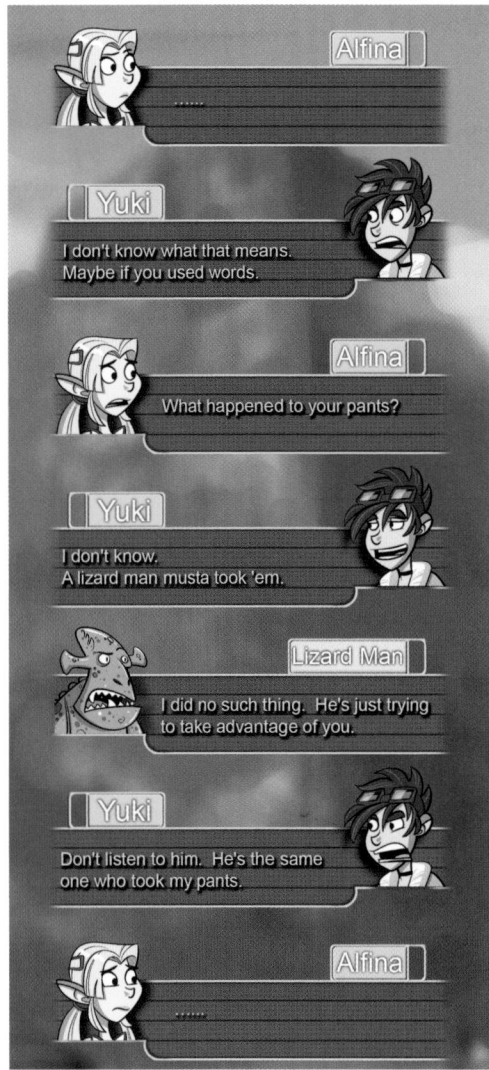

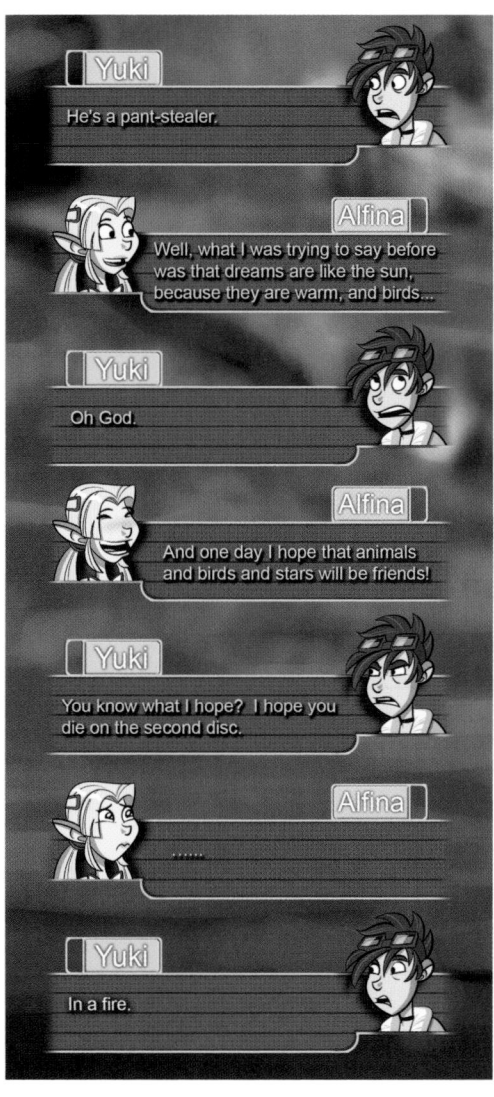

TORMENT UNYIELDING

February 22, 2006 · I don't know if it's something that just isn't being translated correctly, or if there's some basic mismatch between Japanese and American genre tropes that results in this kind of stuff, but the shit these people say is incredible. And it's not the good kind of incredible.

It's been a long time since 2006, though, and the trend is Japanese releases with much more natural language. *Localization* was once synonymous with *translation,* but I tend to use these words to describe two distinct philosophies of approaching the process. *Localization* is when a publisher gives the translator sufficient freedom to interpret the text. *Translation* is the name I have for literary abortions like Grandia III.

OUR SECRET WORLD

February 24, 2006 · Mega Man X is actually a separate branch of the franchise altogether, but I had always assumed that it was the tenth game, because there are so Goddamn many of those things. I was wrong, which happens occasionally. I think that I actually made up the term *junkslut,* which I like, and have gotten a lot of use out of— especially at my drug-fueled orgies. But maybe I'm wrong about that, too, in which case there's no truth anywhere in this comic.

SOMEONE PLEASE CALL SECURITY

February 27, 2006 · Absolutely true, minus the dancing. I had preordered Black to get the demo, but the demo was so nasty that it made me regret having preordered. I'd trudged to the store purely out of a sense of duty—and because he'd called me to come get it—but I didn't even want the Goddamn thing anymore. Everything turned out all right in the end, though. As I mentioned in the post, there was a Cinnabon *just next door*.

A WASTE SENSATION

March 1, 2006 · The game Gabriel is referring to is Sony Online Entertainment's DC Universe Online, but whatever. The important thing here is that after seeing this comic strip, the president of Sony Online Entertainment sent us twelve hundred freshly baked Krispy Kreme doughnuts. We couldn't eat them all, no; we donated the remainder. I made a hell of a run at it, though.

THE FORBIDDEN FRUIT

March 3, 2006 · These books catalog at an extremely high resolution our slow conversion from ridicule, to curiosity, deflection, and then, ultimately, embrace. I wasn't aware of just how granular it was at the time, or how completely we had collected it. It's like that a lot, going through the archive: the sense that I am reading my own diary. Which I basically am.

THE TOME OF SECRETS

March 6, 2006 · I wanted to give the Apple enthusiasts whom we had spent so much time taunting over the years an opportunity to get some enjoyment at my expense. I never mind being the butt of the joke, so long as it's a good joke. In the end, I don't especially care *why* you're laughing, so long as you are—and that we had something to do with it.

THE GAMBLER, PART ONE

March 8, 2006 · Gabriel—the real one, and the figurative one seen above—are both equally obsessed with Kenny Rogers. At work, I can only see the top 30 percent of Gabriel's face over the monitor. But when a Kenny Rogers song is selected by the shuffle algorithm, this head portion can be seen to bob to his steady rhythms.

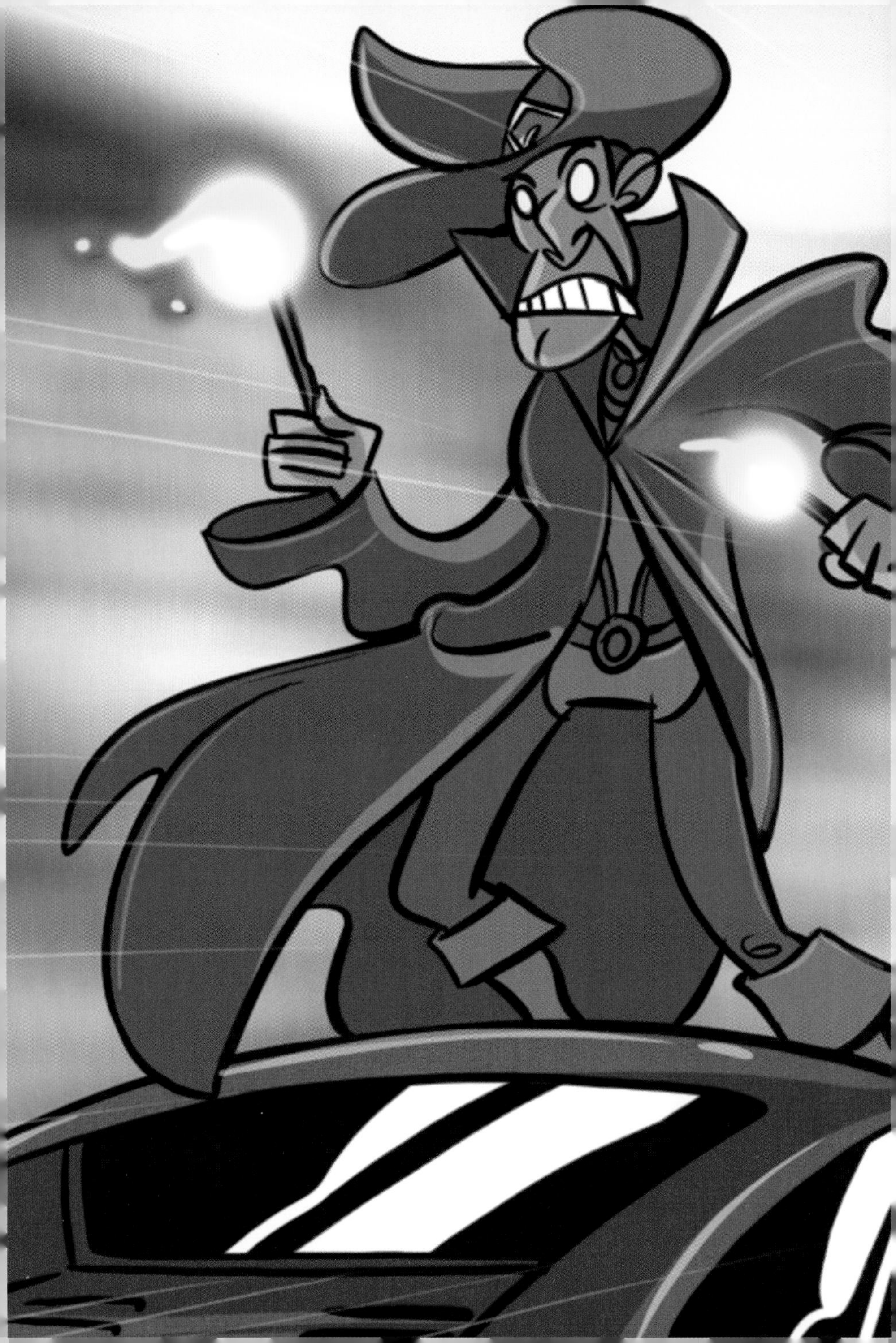

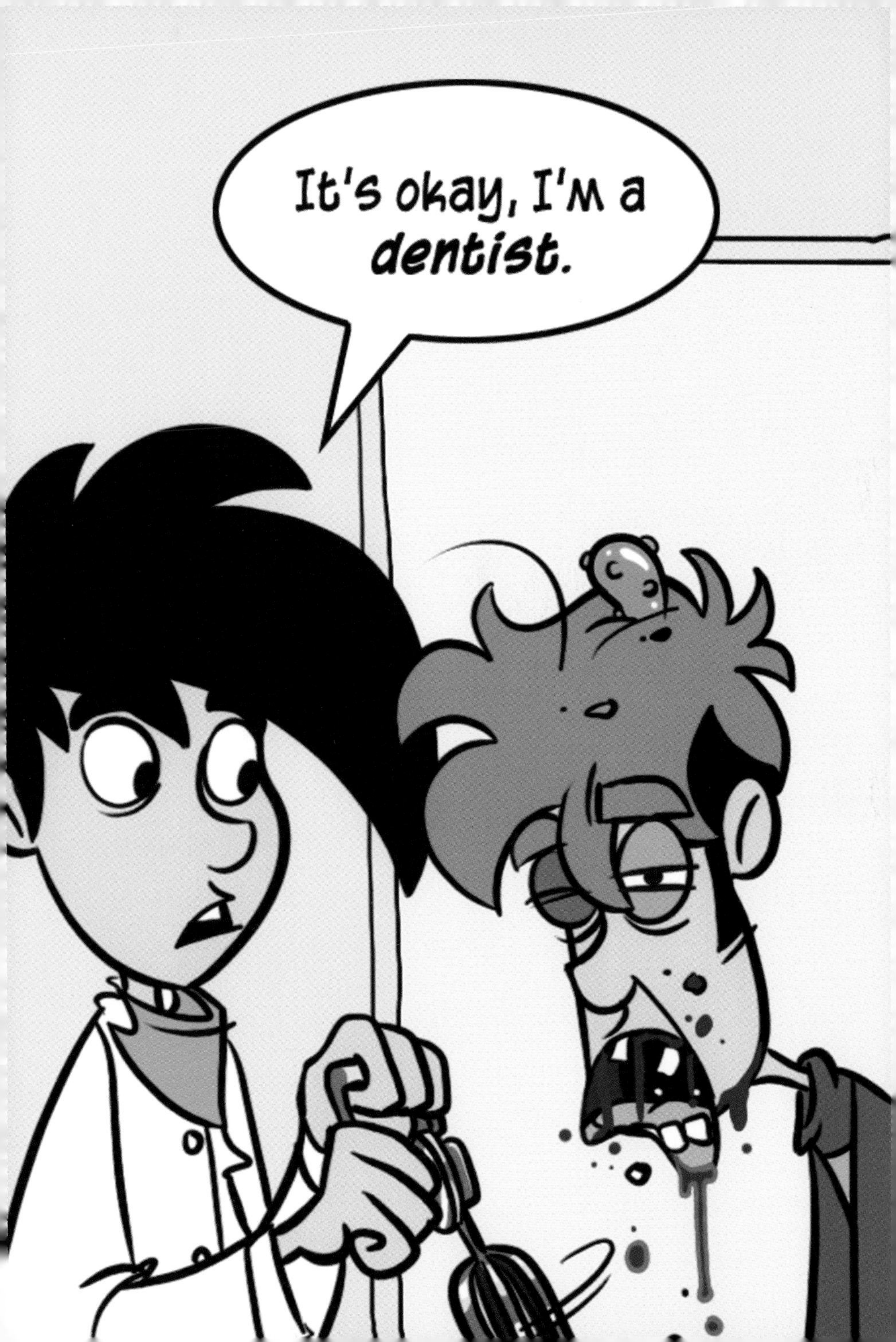
It's okay, I'm a *dentist.*

THE GAMBLER, PART TWO

March 10, 2006 · Kenny Rogers has a chicken restaurant, which you might not have known about. I think they're mostly in Singapore now. Kenny Rogers also has a beverage on the market, one that tastes like salty yogurt. Also, was this *entire exercise* an excuse for Gabriel to draw Kenny Rogers, silvered by the moonlight?

THE GAMBLER, PART THREE

March 13, 2006 · Right about now, I think the silvered-by-the-moonlight hypothesis is looking pretty strong.

In a surprising move this week, Soviet copy protection vendor slash *crime syndicate* Starforce began actively promoting piracy of Stardock's Galactic Civilizations 2.

Randy Pinkwood
Channel 2

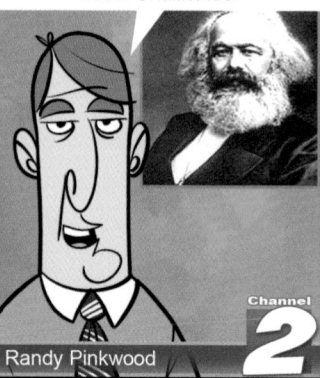

When asked for comment, the reasonable people of the world called their behavior "extortion."

I've never been to Russia, but I did have sex with a girl who said she was a *communist*.

Randy Pinkwood
Channel 2

I don't know if she was serious or not, but she certainly "seized the means of production," if you know what I'm talking about.

And I think you know what I'm talking about.

I'm talking about my *penis*.

Randy Pinkwood
Channel 2

IN LEAGUE WITH DEMONIC FORCES

March 15, 2006 · This was actually pretty strange, all things considered: An employee of DRM factory StarForce thought it would be a hoot to link a bunch of torrents for the recently released Galactic Civilizations II. Stardock (quite famously) doesn't apply intrusive digital rights management schemes, which made that torrent stuff look like some kind of Mafia protection racket. Weird, weird, weird.

Oh, there's Miguel.

What did he say? I can't really hear him.

Let's go say hi.

It's you guys! Thank God! Listen! You gotta get me down!

VIVA DECAPITATION

March 17, 2006 · I like games where you build a place and then things come to live there based on how you built it, the Dungeon Keepers being my favorites. This said, personifying an object whose sole purpose is to be hung from a tree and beaten by children until its guts fall out and kids eat them strikes me as, oh, I don't know. I'm going to go with "odd."

THIS IS WHAT DEMOCRACY LOOKS LIKE

March 20, 2006 · This is back in a big way now, this legal stuff, and at the time of this writing nothing in the California suit has been resolved—it's not currently known whether they're going to make a special regulatory exception for the "unique dangers" of video games, as opposed to movies, music, literature, et cetera. It might help if there was a judge somewhere who had played a video game, ever.

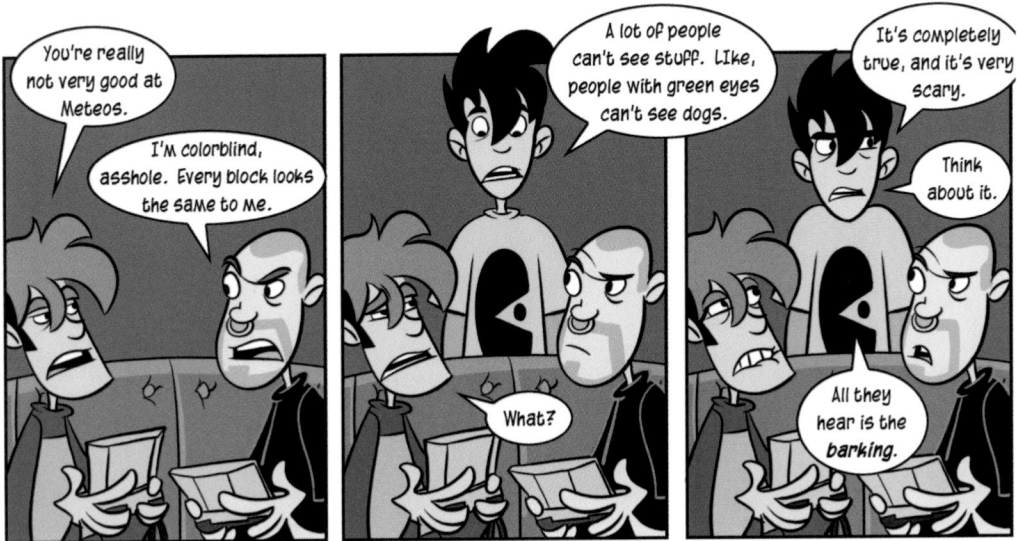

LEAF-EYED SONS OF BITCHES

March 22, 2006 · That's Porkfry up there, which you may or not know, and since it isn't written into the strip I thought I should make a note of it. Fun Porkfry Facts: When his ADHD medication wears off, somewhere around 10 PM, he can speak for twenty-three solid minutes without breathing. Also, he credits Final Fantasy VII with his conversion to Christianity. These things are absolutely true.

THE NOBLE SIR SLEEPINGTON
March 24, 2006 · Gabe was having a hell of a time drawing Gabe's and Tycho's faces from the bottom, because he'd never really done it before, and they aren't really designed to be seen from that angle. The late Mike Wieringo, whom we knew through Scott Kurtz, contacted Gabe immediately and walked him through it. Nice guy.

THE *DOUJINSHI* CODE
March 27, 2006 · *Doujinshi* are (says Wikipedia) "self-published works," which to the West would generally be synonymous with *indie,* but some of these works are self-published because they feature someone else's intellectual property—it would be illegal for a company to publish them. I'm sure there are *doujinshi* where two friends are trying to run a pizza shop and find it difficult, but that's generally not what we saw at anime cons. What we saw at anime cons was a heaving pornucopia of smut.

A BLATANT DISREGARD FOR CANON

March 29, 2006 · I could use this space to explain it to you, to contextualize it, but what's the use? The heart wants what it wants.

FURTHER DEVIATIONS

March 31, 2006 · The accepted truncation here, agreed upon by ourselves and the forum alike, is "Sepoohroth." Kingdom Hearts plays loose with some pretty legendary personae, but when you see what kind of subversion they were getting away with in Epic Mickey, Square's treatment of the Disney canon has a pretty light touch.

LANTERNALIA

April 3, 2006 · This was a surprise to me, too, but I sort of had the idea that if you can draw then you could just draw . . . anything. Like, if you had seen a comic or something, or a character, you could just move your hand around and reproduce it. Not so, says Gabriel. He says that drawing can be quite difficult! I wonder what other obvious things I don't understand.

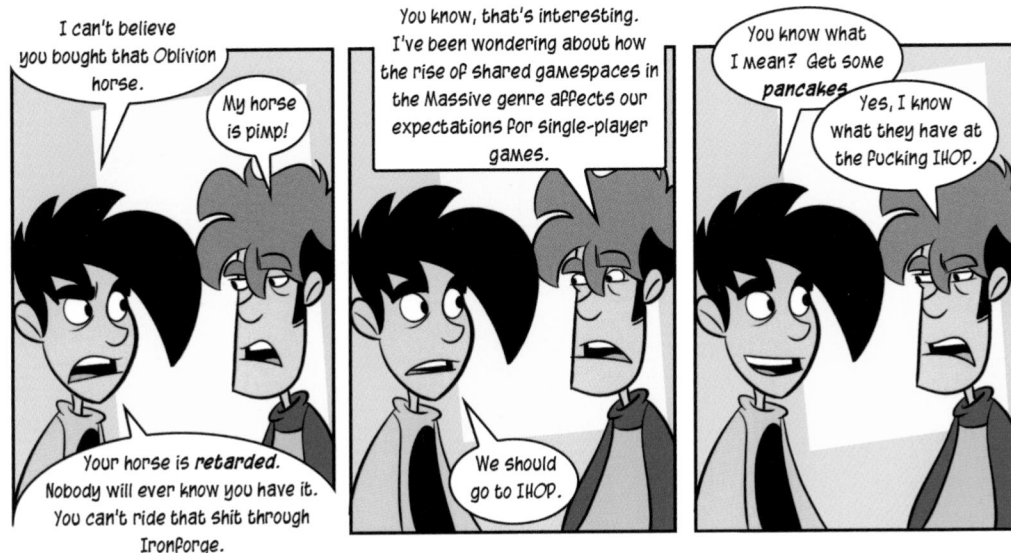

THE ZONE OF PURE BREAKFAST

April 5, 2006 · This comic ought to help you place this book in its proper chronological locale: This comic is about The Elder Scrolls IV, most often referred to by its subtitle Oblivion—and known for its ill-fated Horse Armor. *Horse Armor* would go on to become the shorthand term for what the community deems mean-spirited, mercenary DLC. I've heard, but can't prove, that they made a million dollars off it, which (if you were wondering) might explain why a company would do that.

ON SACKS

April 7, 2006 · Lionhead is a company that was primarily known for having a lot of big ideas that they would discuss at length through speech polyp Peter Molyneux, and then they would release games that did not resemble what they had talked about previously. We didn't entirely understand the thinking behind this acquisition, but if any company needs an injection of chaos it's probably Microsoft.

I HOPE YOU LIKE TEXT

April 10, 2006 · This comic was well received, which surprised me—you can see my hedging there in the very title of the strip. Topically speaking, I had just gotten so tired of the notion—oft-repeated by know-nothing human voids—that Games Workshop had stolen this or that from Blizzard. Blizzard's evolved their franchises significantly as the settings have progressed, but let us be clear. The debt goes entirely in the other direction.

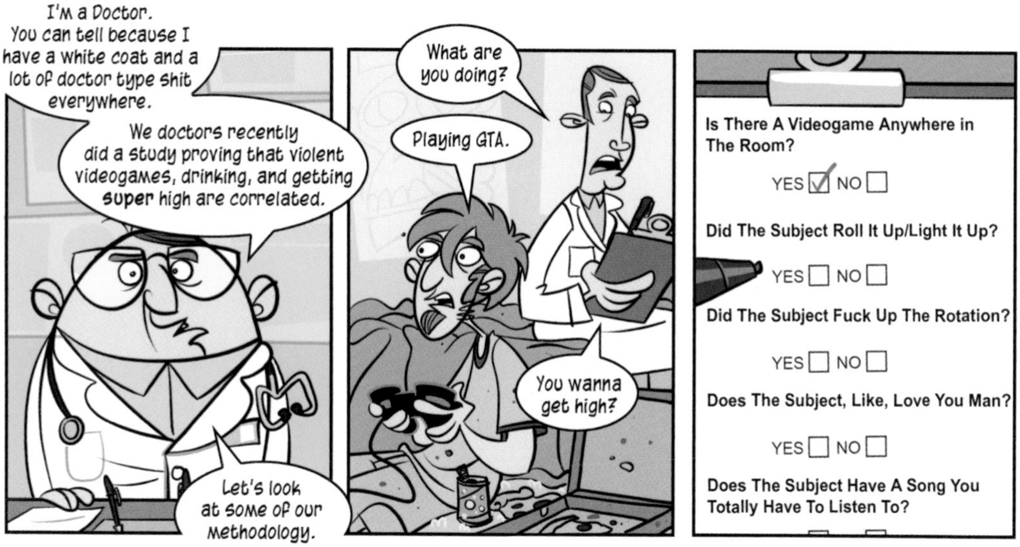
I'm a Doctor. You can tell because I have a white coat and a lot of doctor type shit everywhere.
We doctors recently did a study proving that violent videogames, drinking, and getting super high are correlated.
Let's look at some of our methodology.
What are you doing?
Playing GTA.
You wanna get high?
Is There A Videogame Anywhere in The Room?
YES NO
Did The Subject Roll It Up/Light It Up?
YES NO
Did The Subject Fuck Up The Rotation?
YES NO
Does The Subject, Like, Love You Man?
YES NO
Does The Subject Have A Song You Totally Have To Listen To?

DOCTOR FEELGOOD

April 12, 2006 · There was a "study"—and isn't there always—but there was a *study* that connected playing video games with increased alcohol and marijuana use. What it actually said was that people who play games are more likely to be tolerant of those behaviors, but let's not get hung up on something like actual words! What's crucial is that we get some spooky headlines ginned up to scare the shit out of some moms.

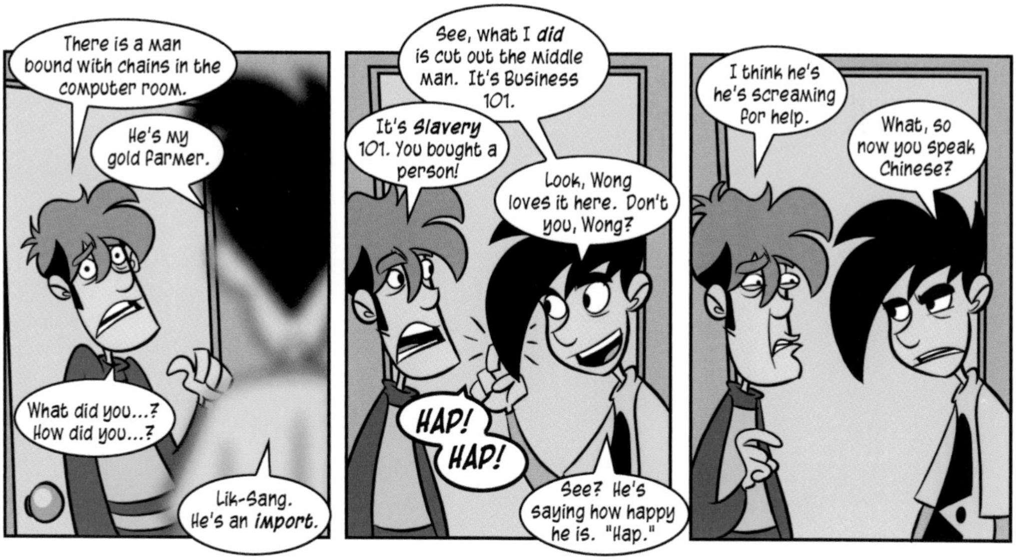
There is a man bound with chains in the computer room.
He's my gold farmer.
What did you...? How did you...?
Lik-Sang. He's an *import*.
See, what I *did* is cut out the middle man. It's Business 101.
It's *Slavery* 101. You bought a person!
Look, Wong loves it here. Don't you, Wong?
HAP! HAP!
See? He's saying how happy he is. "Hap."
I think he's he's screaming for help.
What, so now you speak Chinese?

THE INSUPERABLE BARRIER OF LANGUAGE

April 14, 2006 · Gold-farming sweatshops where people essentially mine virtual resources for pennies and then sell them to a global elite is so fucking cyberpunk I can't stand it. This would be the entire plot of a book written in the early '80s, *except this shit is a real thing that is happening.*

AS SPRING DAWNS

April 17, 2006 · I write this as we're about due for another entry in the greater ardboard Tube Samurai *oeuvre*. I have two full stories, maybe twelve pages apie ore or less ready to go—but projects of that weight aren't really available to us i e normal course. Plus, we never quite know if taking over the site for something xtended like that is okay with you. The way we work this these days is to put up ree project ideas, and let people pick. That's been a fun way to go about it

TREACHERY IN 1080i

April 19, 2006 · Ah, HD-DVD, we hardly knew ye. Well, I guess we did sort of know ye. You were the format with less robust studio support and lower real (as well as theoretical) data densities. You did your best, though; you had pluck. King Kong might not have been a great pack-in, no. But you've been punished for that about as bad as you possibly could have been.

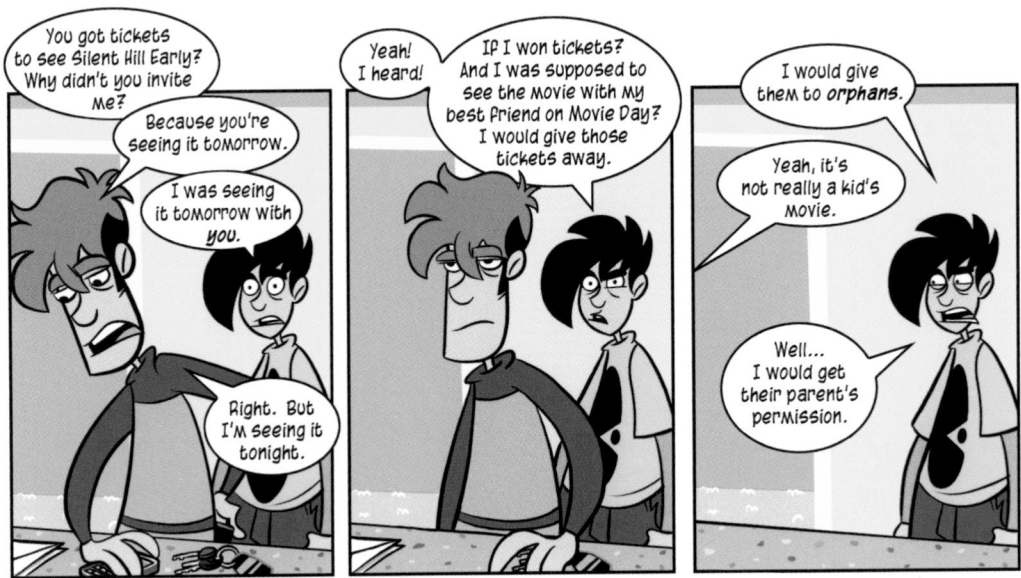

INTERPERSONAL CONFLICT, PHASE ONE

April 21, 2006 · I did win a ticket, that part is true, and Gabriel was angry about it for some reason, which is also true. Every part of this comic, every arc of its emotional contours, is the crystalline essence of truth. When calibrating their truth-detection equipment, engineers are known to calibrate them with this strip's peculiar frequency.

INTERPERSONAL CONFLICT, PHASE TWO

April 24, 2006 · I had mentioned on the site that whenever something good happens to me, like winning movie tickets for example, I feel certain that some kind of *cosmic punishment* is forthcoming. Then I saw the movie I had won tickets to, and knew the sting of fate.

THE BUMP

April 26, 2006 · The bump is terribly, terribly real. When we wrote this strip, I only had two. Now, just feeling around on my body, I count eight.

That's more than there were before.

WHENCE WII

April 28, 2006 · As another indicator of this tome's ancient origins: anger and confusion about Nintendo's insistence on calling their bizarre white brick a "Wii." This was back in the days when we still felt that the desires of the gaming enthusiast were connected in *any way* with a machine's success. Heady times, to be sure.

THAT INFERNAL INDUSTRY

May 1, 2006 · The success or failure of a given product in achieving its aesthetic aims aside, I have nothing but sympathy for those who choose to devote the best years of their lives to the creation of electronic entertainment. It's an often brutal state of affairs, and I'll be happy when my job no longer involves pissing in their mouths.

A FAILURE TO PLAN

May 3, 2006 · Illnesses rip through our office now even worse than they did then. In the time presented here, Gabriel's son (who is named Gabriel, only for reals) had brought some bloodthirsty creature home from day care, and it was weeks until it was flushed completely out. Now we've got two kids apiece, so we spend one out of every three days flat on our backs, unrecognizable fluids shooting out in arcing jets.

HIS DIMINUTIVE MASTER

May 5, 2006 · People must have been able to accomplish these feats, at least some of them, but if even *one* person is able to manage it and then uploads the results to YouTube, the pressure is completely off. I play games for fun. I'm not averse to challenge, but I'm not a masochist. And there's only so many hours in the day.

THE UNMISTAKABLE SCENT

May 8, 2006 · I think I may be cured forever now; two children, a few traumatic raid experiences, and the slow transmutation of World of Warcraft from leisure activity to duty have culminated in something like broad-spectrum aversion therapy. I recognize and even celebrate the game's accomplishments, but that appreciation is sequestered somewhere in a rational reserve of my brain. The belly-fire is completely gone.

THE NOT SO DEARLY DEPARTED

May 9, 2006 · Vanguard stumbled in madness and disarray for years until being released in a gruesome state. It had (and has) neat ideas, though: Novel card-based diplomacy, dual targeting, and card-ass, muhfuckin' *diplomacation* top my personal list.

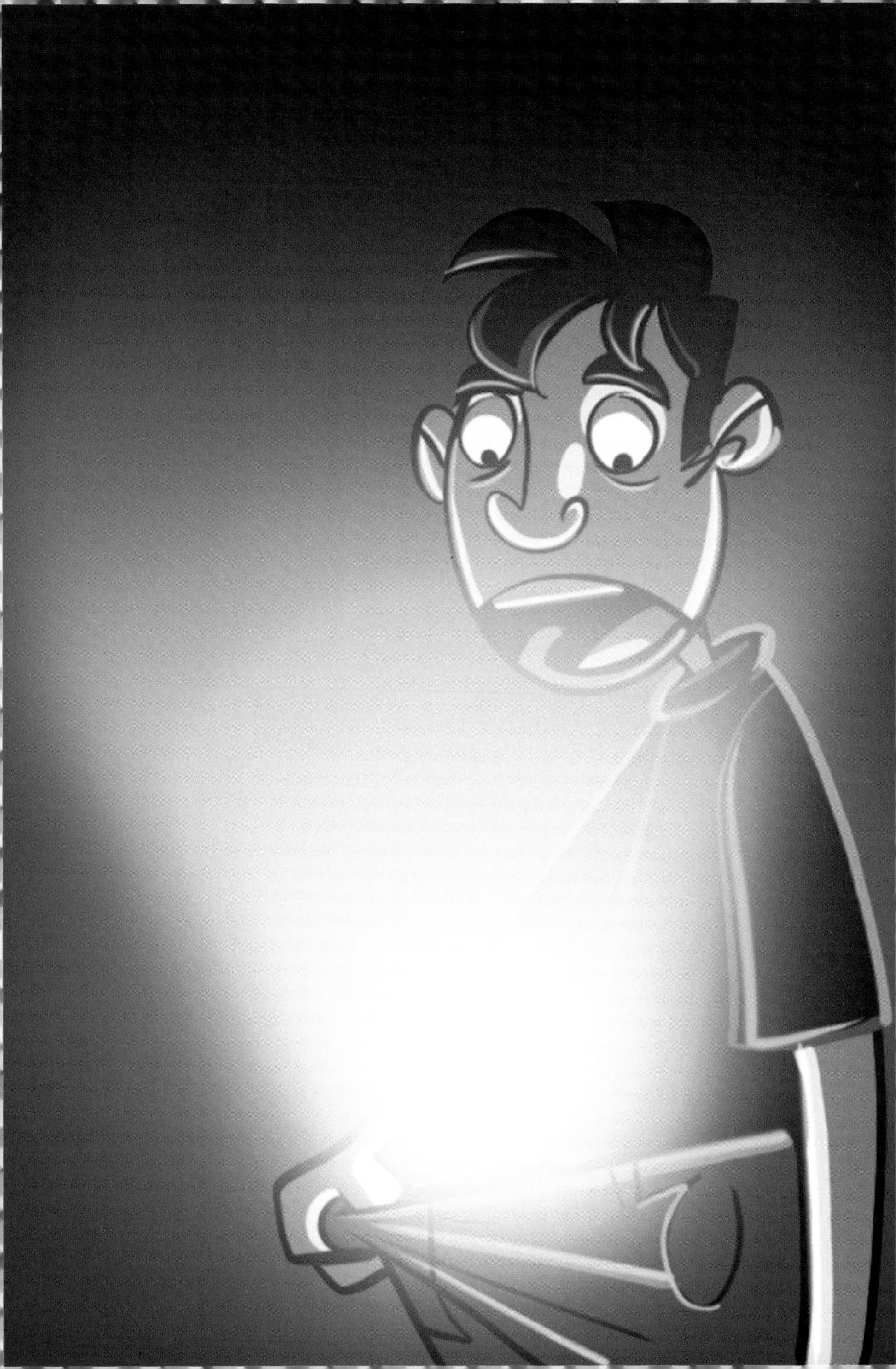

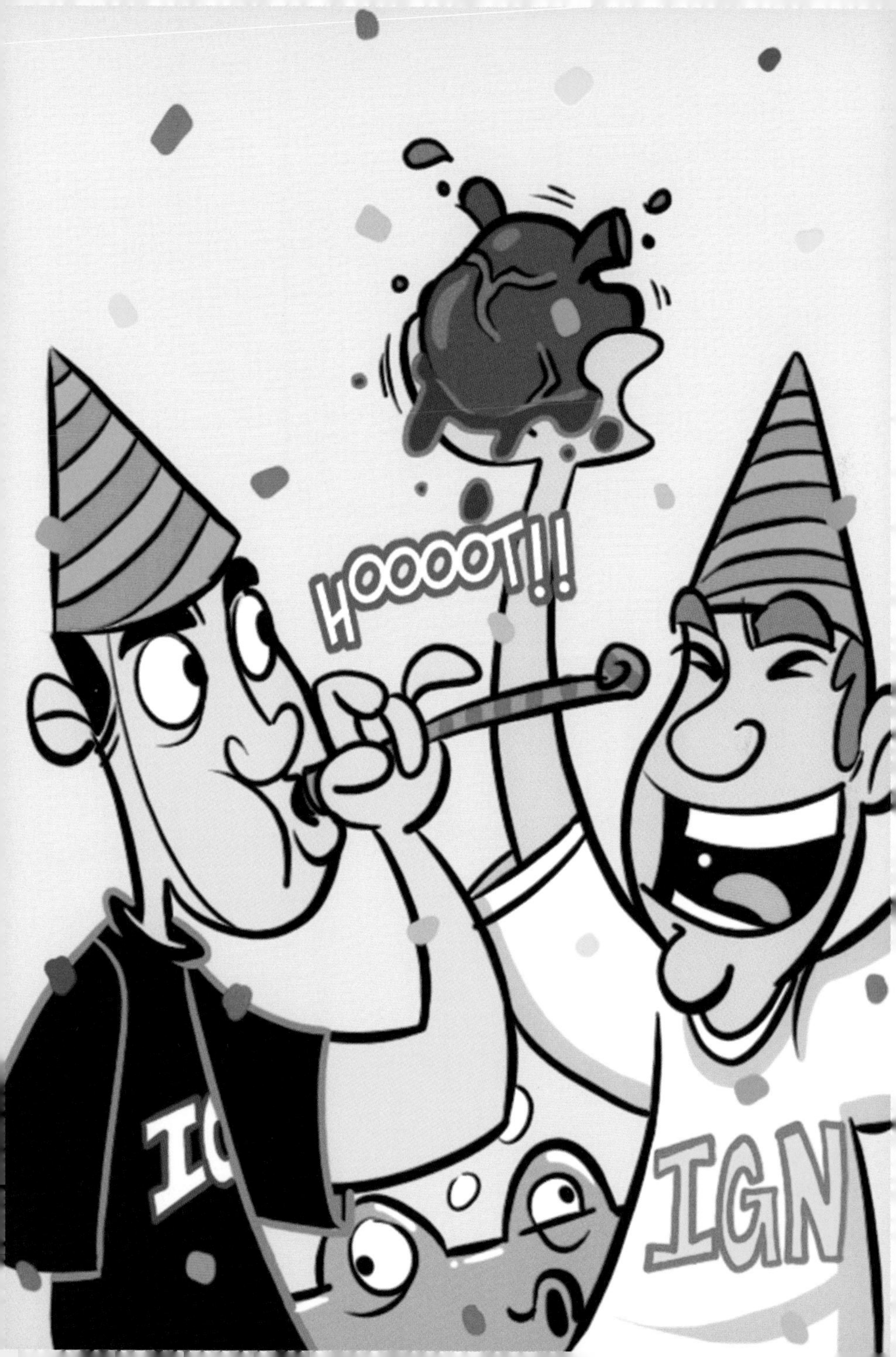
HOOOOT!!
IG
IGN

Gabe and Tycho take in the Metal Gear Solid 4 trailer

E32K6: LOST IN TRANSLATION
May 12, 2006 ·

We were using Alias Sketchbook Pro then, we must have been, because this is the kind of thing you get out of it: The lines are dark and crisp, but with plenty of sketch energy. Anyway, the mustache never made a lot of sense to us, and probably not to a lot of other people who aren't Hideo Kojima. I would love to hear a strong case for why he has that on his face.

KENTIA ALL-STARS
May 15, 2006 · "Kentia" is one of the halls in the Staples Center they hold E3 in, not small by any means, but the term generally acted in those days as a kind of catchall for anything that wasn't absolutely top-tier. Just because a company isn't Activision doesn't mean that they don't have anything to offer the universe, though. You see things like the ones in the strip, sure, but the first time I ever saw NCsoft *they* were in there. Something to think about.

I AM ASHAMED BY PROXY

May 17, 2006 · The line to see the Wii at this E3 was easily the biggest line I have ever seen, at any event I've been to, anywhere. It was so long that as I was winding along its writhing trunk trying to find the end of the Goddamn thing, people currently in the line would appraise me with a haunted expression, nodding side-to-side, mouths open, a silent warning on their lips.

THE SONG OF THE SORCELATOR, PART ONE

May 19, 2006 · *The Song of the Sorcelator* contains some of my favorite *Penny Arcade* strips, and several of my favorite individual lines. We would approach the "sorcelator" material more directly later—think ye upon Witchaloks, and their Wolfoid servitors—but *man.* This was so much fun.

THE SONG OF THE SORCELATOR, PART TWO

May 22, 2006 · Of course he likes it. OF COURSE. But then, we explicitly made it to be so bad that it was awesome in a way. My friend Mike Fehlauer (whom you might have seen in the show; he's the one with the sword) calls this kind of good badness "Van Art Fantasy," which is a nice mental container for this idea. If it were airbrushed on the side of a van, would it be "sweet"? Sorcelator stuff must meet this standard.

THE SONG OF THE SORCELATOR, PART THREE

May 24, 2006 · We attended a science-fiction and fantasy readers convention around here called Foolscap, which was one of the more interesting events I've ever attended. When most of what you attend are events like Sakura-Con or San Diego Comic-Con or PAX, the scale defines a lot of things about the show. Readiation is a nod to those cons, the readers, and the awesome local authors and shops creating unique culture anywhere it will take root.

THE SONG OF THE SORCELATOR, PART FOUR

May 26, 2006 · You might know it, but you also might not, so I should tell you. In the Elemenstor fiction, the *fictional* fiction of the Elemenstors, these wizards run around with animate furniture beasts called furniliars. You never, never create a furniliar out of a nightstand, because . . . well . . . you just don't do that.

THE SONG OF THE SORCELATOR, PART FIVE

May 29, 2006 · SERVES YOU RIGHT. Now die! Die with your monstrous God!

TYCHO EVER-LISTENING

May 31, 2006 · We are sometimes able to teach cartooning at a grade school about an hour south of the office. As the "cool uncles" of Mrs. Eriksen's third-grade class, we just come in with pencils and paper with comic frames on it and talk about how you can build a comic from three parts, just like a snowman. In our example strip, monkeys feature prominently. You can't say we don't know our audience.

THE SAME AS IT EVER WAS

June 2, 2006 · The "big story" this time was that young men were using their PSPs to look at girl parts over the school's unsecured (!) wireless-fi. I chose this title because it really *is* the same as always. Kids are always pulling shit like this; this is very much the realm of *Dog Bites Man.* Or boy, in this case. I also chose it because that's the name of the second House of Pain album.

ALMOST STARTLINGLY RETRO

June 5, 2006 · Ping-Pong (table tennis, if you're nasty) is very serious business around here. Every week, there are matches to determine one's rank. These ranks are used to determine who gets to play in matches against other companies, but they also determine your worth as a human being. Rockstar's Table Tennis catalyzed this entire ritual.

WHOOPSIE DAISY

June 7, 2006 · It's hard to imagine that something like this could go on, but it happened frequently with paintings as well: paintings beneath paintings, all piled up on the same frame. I would think of that original tape as a kind of treasure, but if you're George Lucas, maybe there's no spiritual component. You know? He was there at its genesis, so there's no mysticism associated with it. Maybe that's just something he owns.

THE ENEMY

June 9, 2006 · I know that in his capacity as a retail manipulator—before he rose to Internet Godhood—our own Gabriel would often amuse himself at the expense of his customers. These people do work in stores, and they do their best, but it's got to be incredibly boring sometimes and I don't blame them for finding amusement where they can.

THE ADVERSARY

June 12, 2006 · Like so many of the words from a youth spent in church plays, church choirs, and church camps, *adversary* has retained every cubic centimeter of its explosive payload. *The Adversary* is just another way of saying *Satan the Devil,* but it's got much greater subtlety and power. Satan is a red dude, rubbing his hands together, jumping back and forth from hoof to onyx hoof. The nameless Adversary inspires substantially more dread.

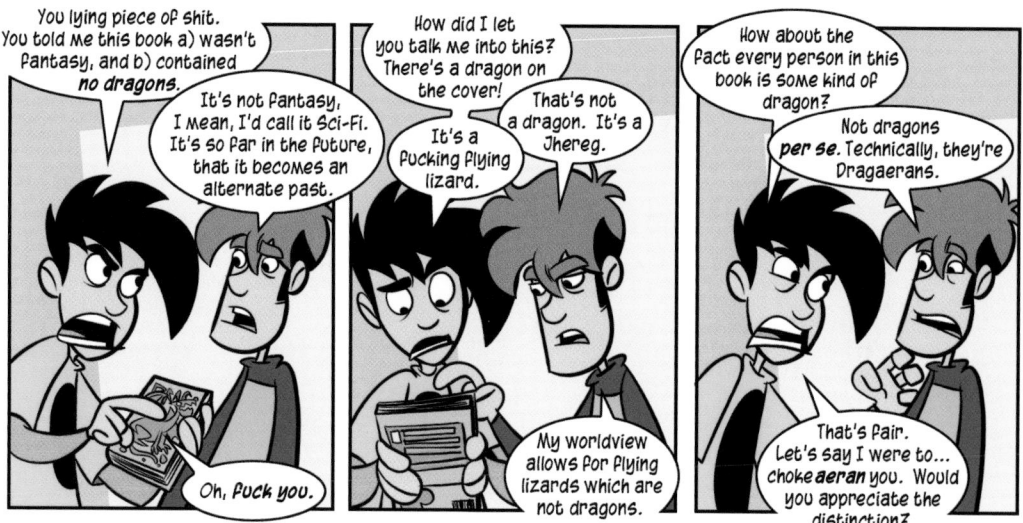

FINE DISTINCTIONS

June 14, 2006 · I brought Steven Brust's Vlad Taltos books to his attention because they are awesome, and this is the thanks I get. If the old models hold, ten years from now he'll bring me the first book—*Jhereg*—and tell me it's "really great" and that I should consider reading it. After stewing in this "revelation" for a brief period, no longer than ten seconds, I will deliver a brutal chop to his trachea.

TREACHERY MANIFEST

June 16, 2006 · Okay, so maybe they're not doing that. But Blizzard doesn't have that many contexts to set games *in,* so figuring out what they're doing next usually isn't that hard. Maybe there's still hope for this thing; I think my friends are probably tired of hearing all of my "awesome" ideas for this wholly imaginary MMO. There are usually three empty glasses in front of me already when I start talking about *squad level* and *carrier crafting,* and things don't improve much from there.

THE THROES OF DATA ADDICTION

June 19, 2006 · This was especially crazy, I thought. No, not trying to track people's gamerscore when you're kicking it in *frozen foods,* although that does seem to express a certain mania. I mean Live Anywhere. You can see from this comic, delivered in June 2006, that it took them four more years to deliver anything of the sort—and then on a phone most people don't have.

GREMLINS ARE A RICH SOURCE OF GREMLINIUM

June 21, 2006 · I described it as "shabby" in that day's post that Blizzard relies on BitTorrent to distribute their updates, and that hasn't stopped being true, but with as many subscribers as they have now those files come down pretty Goddamn fast.

ALWAYS REMEMBER THERE ARE TWO OF US

June 23, 2006 · Stephen Totilo, when he was still defining gaming journalism with his writing at MTV Multiplayer, cooked up a list of the Ten Most Influential Gamers of All Time. Gabriel and I were situated at the top of this list, as The Advocates. This made us feel like special dudes for ten consecutive seconds, and then we resumed our standard policy of intense self-loathing.

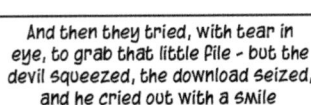

OPEN MIC NIGHT

June 26, 2006 · I don't believe this kind of thing as a blanket principle anymore, but that's because (in the intervening period) I've seen it work well. This was back when they were still trying to figure out what people would endure, with their Horse Armor and their fifteen-dollar map packs for GRAW. I'm incredibly picky about when I choose to support the model; I buy many more complete games from the service than I do add-ons.

MEN ARE FROM KRYPTON

June 28, 2006 · I think you and I may be equally confused about the genesis of this strip, but I may be able to reconstruct a portion of it. *Superman Returns* was just coming out, which I liked a lot actually, and we were writing the strip too close to lunchtime. We try to avoid this, because those comics tend to be *about* food—and the closer lunchtime is, the more about food these strips are. Look up 2004's strip "Lock Your Doors" for the most obvious example.

SUMMER ROAD EPIC, PART ONE

June 30, 2006 · From that day's post:

Whenever I was not beneath the extension cord's downward arc, my father had a passion for "improving" me, though of course this was the stated goal for both processes. His technique was not unlike how a man might introduce a mongoose to a cobra, with the thinking that one of them would be "educated" by the experience. One of them would, it was assumed, be so educated that they would cease to exist. But this was the authentic method of wilderness learning, the true schooling we were all denied when "liberals" built cities and forced men to live within, eschewing bows.

I preferred primary edumacation to Summer Break, as during the summer I had no walking access to a library. I had seen "Time Enough At Last" by then, and time away from a significant concentration of books was not something I could bear on account of the significant Goddamn dangers. No, it was time to pile into the shitwagon and drive up the asshole of Hell. We always had a Bible, and that was a book, and from it I did derive the comfort that men have pulled from it for centuries. I never saw either of them read it. I assumed at the time that it was there in case one of their psychotic "activities" resulted in my death, and they needed to mock up some impromptu last rites.

My parents would drive us to some fucking mudhole in the middle of nowhere, a hundred miles from the nearest shantytown. We'd be crying, up to our asses in mud, Mom would buy some kind of mud pot from the gift shop. My dad would pipe up with something about how this mud had magic properties or was the biggest mudhole, or some other ahistorical bullshit, and this was clearly meant to heighten the already intense pleasure of our mud experience.

The lake we would sometimes travel to, and I think they called it a lake because it had not completely evaporated, was clearly home to toxic mutants. As dangerous as that sounds, this was not the primary concern, for this area of Washington was famous for its rattlesnakes. I don't mean they had a rattlesnake exhibit where you could see them inside a cage, and then emerge from that dark zoo, the sun on your face, in a land blessed and free of them. No, the people in "them parts" are proud of these things. There is a sign by the main thoroughfare that says "Watch Out for Mister Shakes!" who is apparently famous not only for being a snake but for being a very large and dangerous, free roaming fucking man-eating snake. It was my presumption as a young man that he was called Mister Shakes both a) as a courtesy, i.e., "Please don't bite my fucking ass, Mister Shakes!" and also because of the rattling you might hear before he slunk from the grass to murder you. I understand now with the wisdom of many years that the shakes they referred to describe the strong spasms associated with their thick, (sometimes) black venom.

And the food out there on the frontier. Jesus Christ. Eating at whatever rat trap happened to be attached to the gas station we just coasted into. Plate heaped high with fried hair. Warm cylinder of milk pulled from whatever animal happened to be pregnant at the time. So, no. He can rattle his keys all day, if he would like. I'm not going to suit up and get in the car just so I can drink cat milk, eat hair, and get killed by the king of fucking snakes.

(CW)TB out.

me in front of big-ass grape, this was the biggest grape i had ever seen!

Its feline wisdom was almost palpable.

SUMMER ROAD EPIC, PART TWO

July 3, 2006 · I actually did see something cool on a trip, something really cool: a wax museum. Seeing ancient figures or torture implements, obviously there's a spook factor, but for some reason the statues of people still living were more terrifying. Also, at the end there was a *real person* who was not a statue, and they would jump out at you and say BOOGA BOOGA BOOGA!

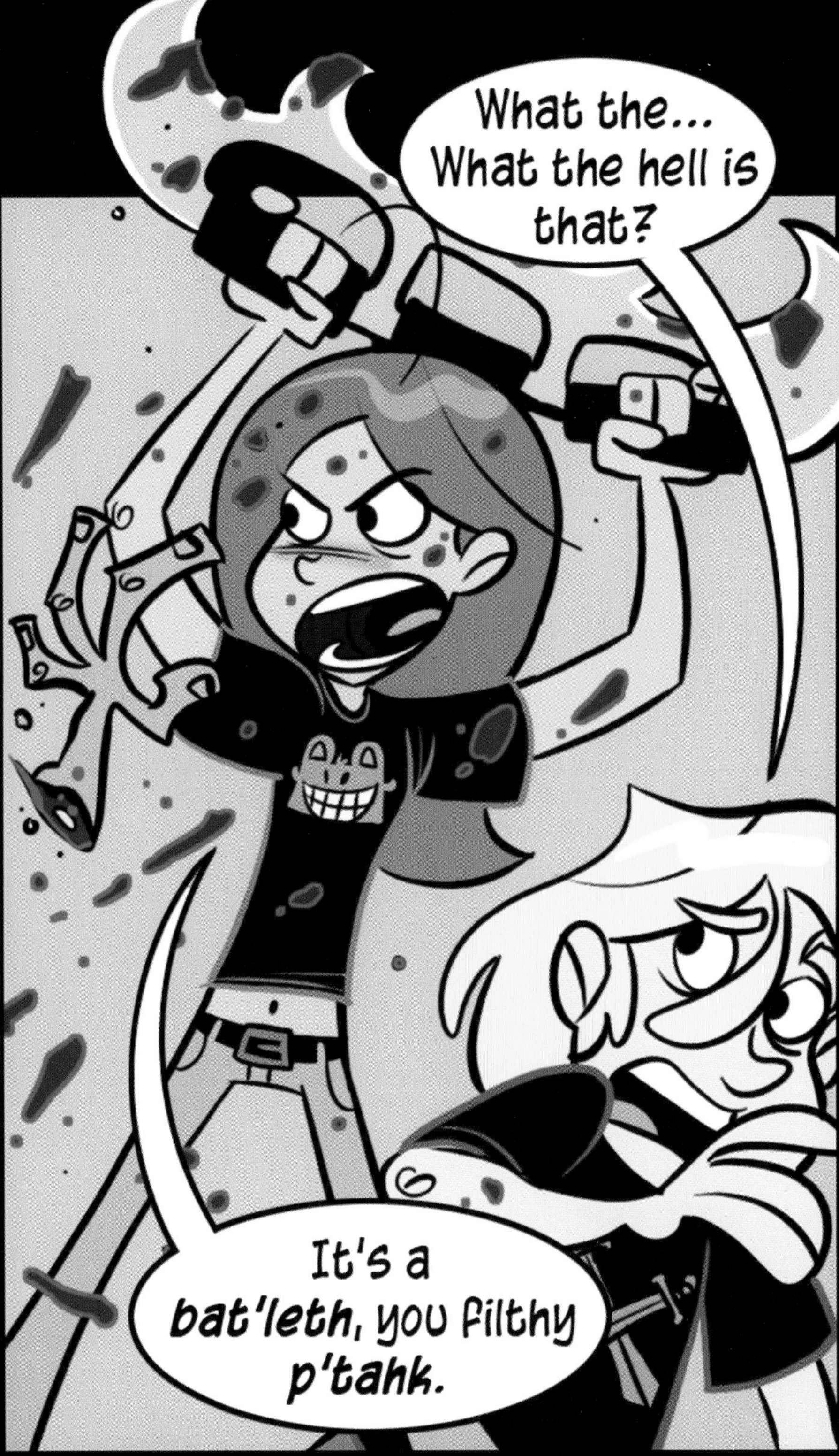
What the... What the hell is that?
It's a *bat'leth*, you filthy *p'tahk*.

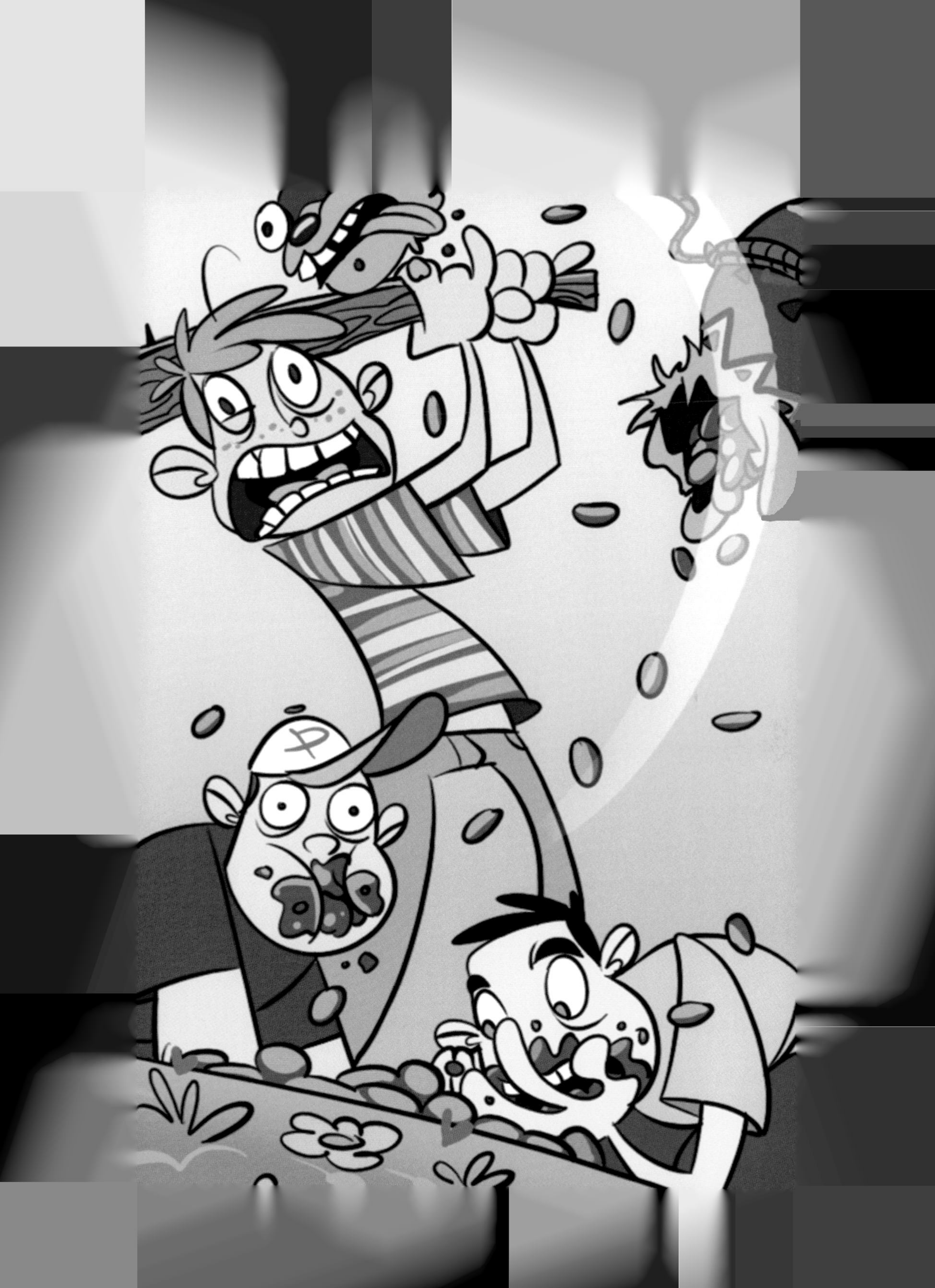

THIRD GRADE GOLD, WILD STYLES

July 5, 2006 · You saw earlier that we teach cartooning on occasion, not frequently enough for my taste, but after we'd done the class Mrs. Eriksen sent us some of the students' work in the mail. You can see here the template we had them filling out before, with MY CARTOON proudly emblazoned, and the action-packed dance floor conflicts that sometimes erupt there.

THIRD GRADE GOLD, THE SECRET

July 7, 2006 · Tycho's line in the first panel is "Tell what?" but it's hard to see in a third grader's hand, there. This was one of the other three templates we used, and we thought it might help the kids who aren't as comfortable rendering in the blank panels. We loved the idea of a secret pig, one that needed to be kept hidden from the parents. This strip might even be autobiographical; we didn't ask.

BETTER LATE THAN NEVER

July 10, 2006 · I actually ended up liking Too Human a lot, a rarity among game enthusiasts. I'm not going to tell you it was perfect, but I had a lot of fun with it, enjoyed its take on quick melee striking, and was completely enraptured by its approach to Norse mythology. I'd gladly play two more of those, not that I'll ever get the chance.

A WIDER PERSPECTIVE ON FLAVOR

July 12, 2006 · I can't remember my passwords, either, and I'm completely incapable of making a "secret question" that's worth a good Goddamn. I'm kind of paranoid about this stuff, and as a result my passwords are all complete nonsense. If it's a site I don't visit every day, I have to use the password retrieval mechanism pretty much every time.

F(R)ICTION

July 14, 2006 · Rainbow Six: Vegas is not a documentary! This has got to be one of those generational things.

TRANSFORMERS TRANSFIGURED

July 17, 2006 · It wasn't that bad, actually. The changes they made to the iconic robots were necessary, in some ways. As much as I like the cartoon, *and I do like the cartoooon,* it has a tiny Walkman that could transform into a big-ass robot. It might be kinda hard to sell something like that in an actual movie.

Comic Con 2006

Gooood afternoon from the cockpit, ladies and gentlemen. This is your captain, Captain Steve. We're looking at aboooouut three hours down to San Diego today, we're expecting a smooooth flight, I have turned off the fasten seat belts sign and you are free to move about the cabin. I have a ball of heroin about the size of a monkey's fist jammed straight up my asshole. Beauutiful weather down there, clear skies, and seventy eight degrees...

DO YOU HEAR WHAT I HEAR

July 19, 2006 · We'd brought a Tablet PC down with us to do the week's work on, the same one that we'd used at E3, except now it was completely F'd in or around the A region. We could apply the text, as you see, but all the tablet functionality had evaporated. Gabe drew the strip on a napkin with a ballpoint pen from the lounge. I supplied the empty martini glass.

SKETCHSTRAVAGANZA

July 21, 2006 · Sketching on the tables at cons is a long-standing *Penny Arcade* tradition, one that took the main stage when our laptop became incorrigible. This is only a small portion of a table here, but one of our earlier books includes a gallery of them covering a few years. I don't remember which one has it. You'd think I would; I did write them all.

HUNS AT THE GATES OF CANON
July 24, 2006 · The third strip in our "broken laptop" series is a response to the substantial gradient of *Star Wars* cosplay we saw that year. *Star Wars* is so vast conceptually that at a show like Comic-Con, it's often used as an element of an overall costume: 2006 saw both a Green Lantern Jedi, which I could *kind of* see, and also an Orthodox Jewish Jedi, which is something I had not imagined previously.

ADMONISHMENTS: VIEWSONIC

July 26, 2006 · It's really only on trips that we take time to read actual print gaming magazines, when we are in mid-flight and have no access to the Earth or its flitting data packets. That's when we were exposed to this advertisement and irrevocably harmed. Nowadays you can just log on or whatever from the plane. This was 2006, though. Two thousand six!

We were flying home on a pteranodon.

TURNABOUT

July 28, 2006 · LocoRoco was a lot of fun, I thought. I loved the crisp art on that beautiful screen—but I was then, as always, looking for any excuse to get my PSP out and play it. Ultimately, I think I preferred Rolando to LocoRoco, the iPhone's approach to tiltable organisms. It had sharp puzzles, and a cute look, but it's also one of the first iPhone games I really played and took seriously. I remember it with joy; maybe after I'm done writing this book, I'll put it back on there.

THE THREE ES

July 31, 2006 · Of course, E3 is back now, and not as the half measure it was when it returned initially but as the uncontrollable, ridiculously unmanageable venture it was when they originally decided to put it out to pasture. It's the reversal of what appeared to be the natural trend: a trend toward smaller shows, dedicated to specific publishers or types of attendee.

TWISP & CATSBY IN: THE LAND OF UPP
August 1, 2006 ·
This balloon person is Eric Burns, of the blog Websnark. While still in active production, his blog was crucial reading for followers of webcomic trends—but good Lord, can that guy talk. I would get the point he was trying to make, find it persuasive and well written, and then discover that there were still another two thousand words left.
It's like, man, listen. I've got *shit* to do.

BLACK DIARY RETRIEVALS: THE OLD NEIGHBORHOOD

There was a period of time, perhaps even a discrete era, where battling each other with Nerf weaponry was encouraged and even expected. Couple this with our general obsession with noir (which saw a voice in the Automata pieces), and we sort of couldn't avoid making a comic like this. I think he did a really good job on it, but after it was finished, we recognized at some level that it was so radically different from a normal update that we weren't quite comfortable making it the strip for that day. I wanted to track it down though and include it in the book, because it still appeals to me.

And I really, really like the name.

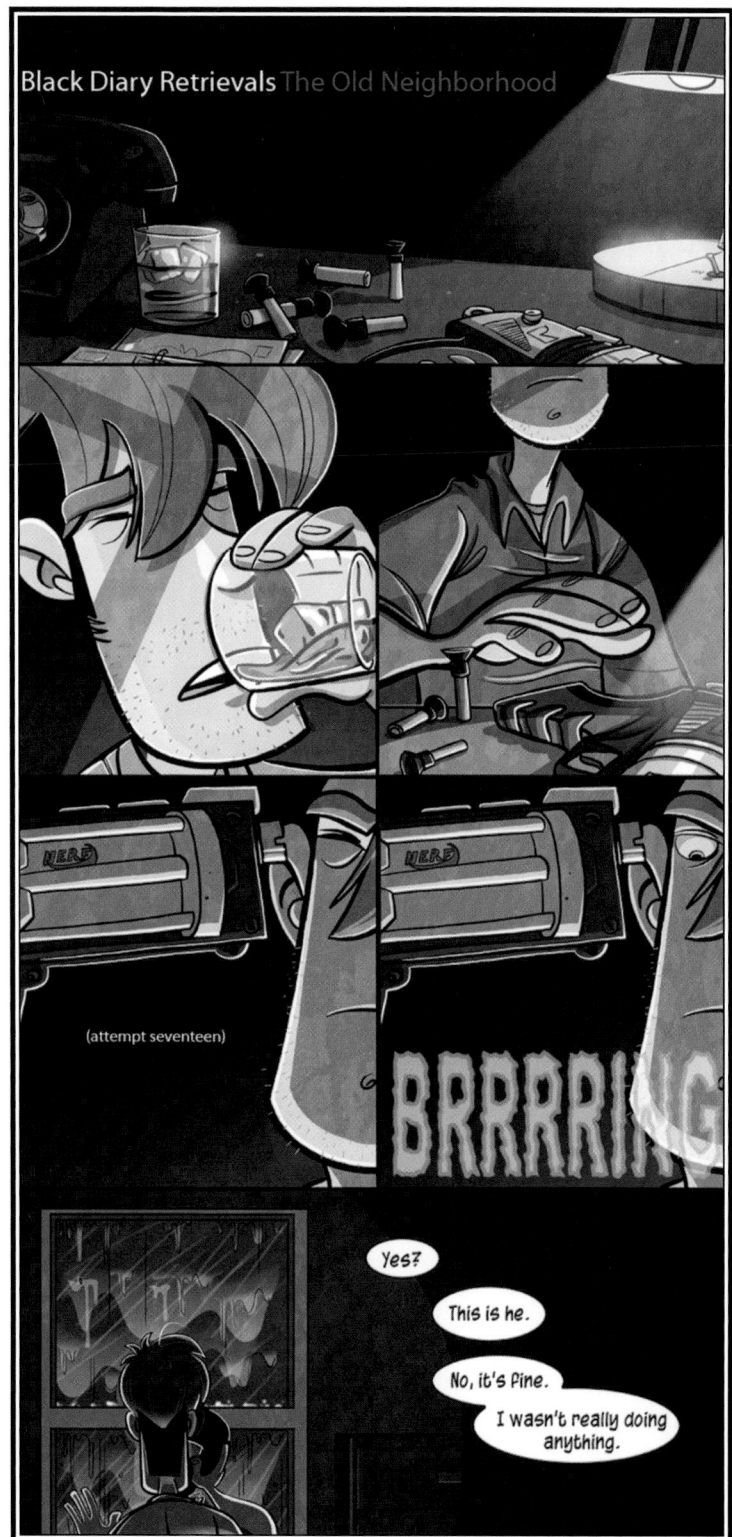

THE ECOLOGY OF THE SUBURBAN THUG

August 4, 2006 · I don't actually blame K-Real for being enthusiastic about Paul Wall's "Sittin' Sidewayz," because we are (ourselves) enthusiasts. Saints Row thugged so hard it was hard to take it seriously, though. Maybe that was the point; maybe it was supposed to be the epic, writ-large, marble-relief *version* of timeless gangsterism. If so, I apologize.

MAN'S INHUMANITY TO MAN

August 7, 2006 · I got signed up for something called "payment insurance" on an appliance we'd paid for up front, that is to say, *there were no payments to pay,* let alone ones that needed insurance. That's a pretty good trick, all told: a new genre of usury, the "payment payment." Goddamn necromancers.

ARMADEADDON: DARK GENESIS

August 9, 2006 · We were obsessed with Dead Rising then—just the demo, not the whole game. We didn't like the whole game for some reason. Well, not just *some* reason. The reason is that the structures they put in place to assure multiple interesting playthroughs, the importance of actual *time,* was something we found incredibly stressful.

ARMADEADDON: THE BLACK ORCHARD

August 11, 2006 · We tuck in Charles whenever we can. But back to Dead Rising. We actually liked Dead Rising 2: Case 0 better than either the full game *or* the original demo. The game wasn't especially long, quite by design, so replaying it wasn't onerous—it was virtually an assumption. It took much of the heat off, and let you iterate quickly and reap the rewards.

ARMADEADDON: BLADE PRINCESS

August 14, 2006 · I can't keep my ass *out* of the House of Cutlery! And now I have a *son* who is just as enamored of its stalwart guardian armor and its warped alien blades sleeping beneath glass. Plus, at our mall, it's right across from See's Candies. I can path quite happily between these two points until Brenna has completed whatever *real* task we came there to do.

ARMADEADDON: SUNDERED UNION

August 16, 2006 · Cowering there beside Annarchy is Galahad, her boyfriend from an earlier series, and many people didn't like that he was actually kind of useless in a zombie infestation scenario. There was some identification with him, perhaps, that we didn't honor. I want to come back to Galahad—I planted the seed of it at the end of this series—but Gabe won't let me.

ARMADEADDON: FLESH HARVEST

August 18, 2006 · The whole idea of the Armadeaddon story line was to see precisely how much fanservice we could compress into each panel: how many tangible rewards we could glom together for the *Penny Arcade* reader with archivist tendencies. A lot, it turns out. Seriously, though. Like, a serious super lot for reals.

ARMADEADDON: BITTER CUP

August 21, 2006 · Let's just say "YUCK" and move on, together, without looking back.

ARMADEADDON: OMINOUS MONIKER

August 23, 2006 · Jim, a "character" who made a single appearance five years ago, seemed like the ultimate nod to the longtime enthusiast. Jim also pops up in On the Rain-Slick Precipice of Darkness for much the same reason. The idea that Gabe and Tycho (as characters) once had a peer of *any* kind, as opposed to a sequence of human props that are necessary for specific jokes, is something I want to investigate further.

ARMADEADDON: GRIM EXODUS

August 25, 2006 · I have a very high opinion of the sixth panel here, where an oblivious Gabriel chows on a cinnamon roll while the fate of his tender brain is decided. And then, in one last sliver of self-referential fanservice, the Tycho Zombie from way, way back—all the way back to our tenth month in operation—dishes up one last miserable backward glance.

ARMADEADDON: EPILOGUE

August 28, 2006 · This is what I was talking about before—the second panel, here. Obviously Gabe needs some "pantz" (as per the first panel of "Ominous Moniker" on page 81), and a non-sequitur bit of maudlin sentimentality at the end of a story this ridiculous seemed crucial. But the glimpse of Galahad, with his mind earnestly focused on learning the language of a nonexistent interstellar aggressor race, seems like it could go somewhere good.

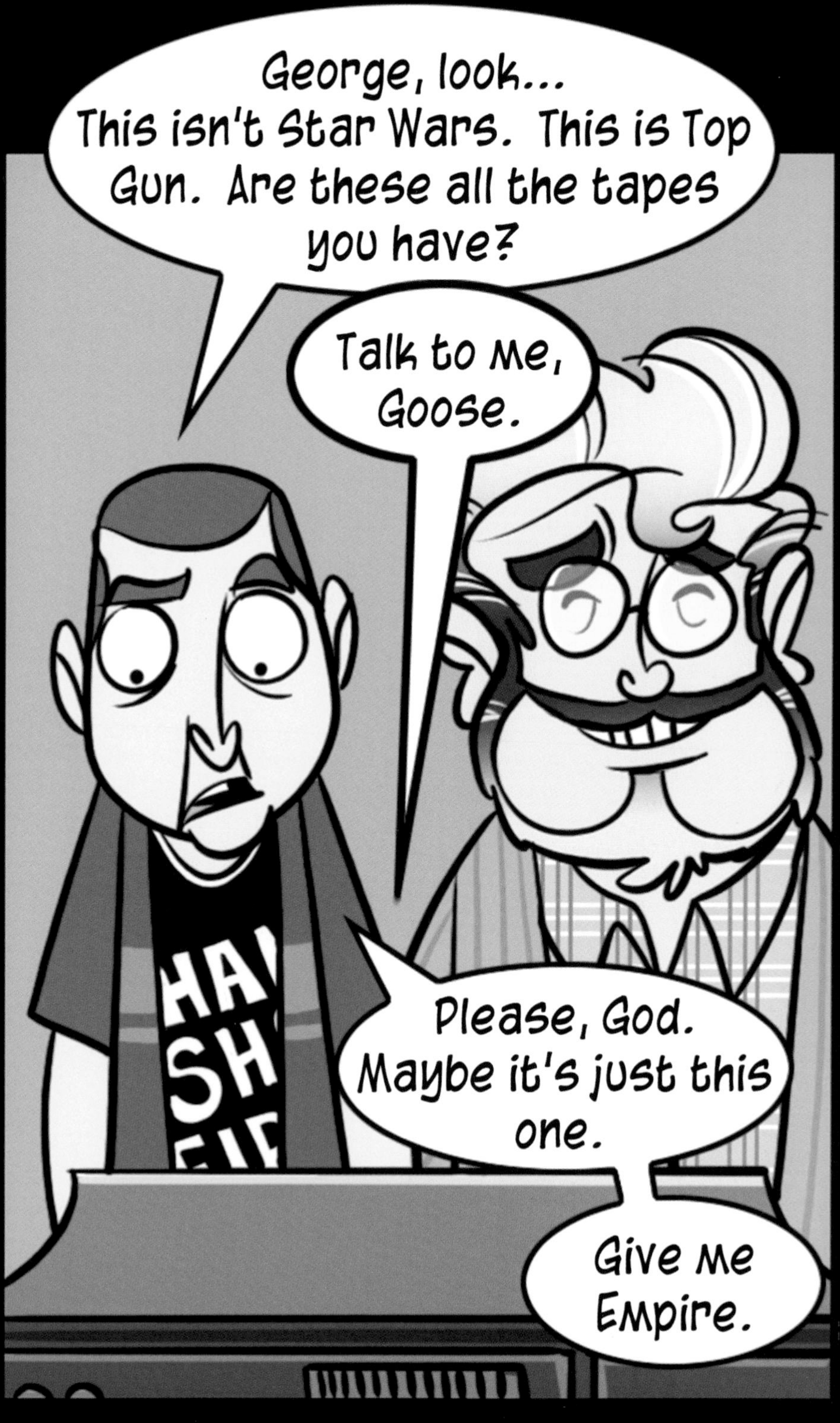
George, look... This isn't Star Wars. This is Top Gun. Are these all the tapes you have?
Talk to me, Goose.
Please, God. Maybe it's just this one.
Give me Empire.

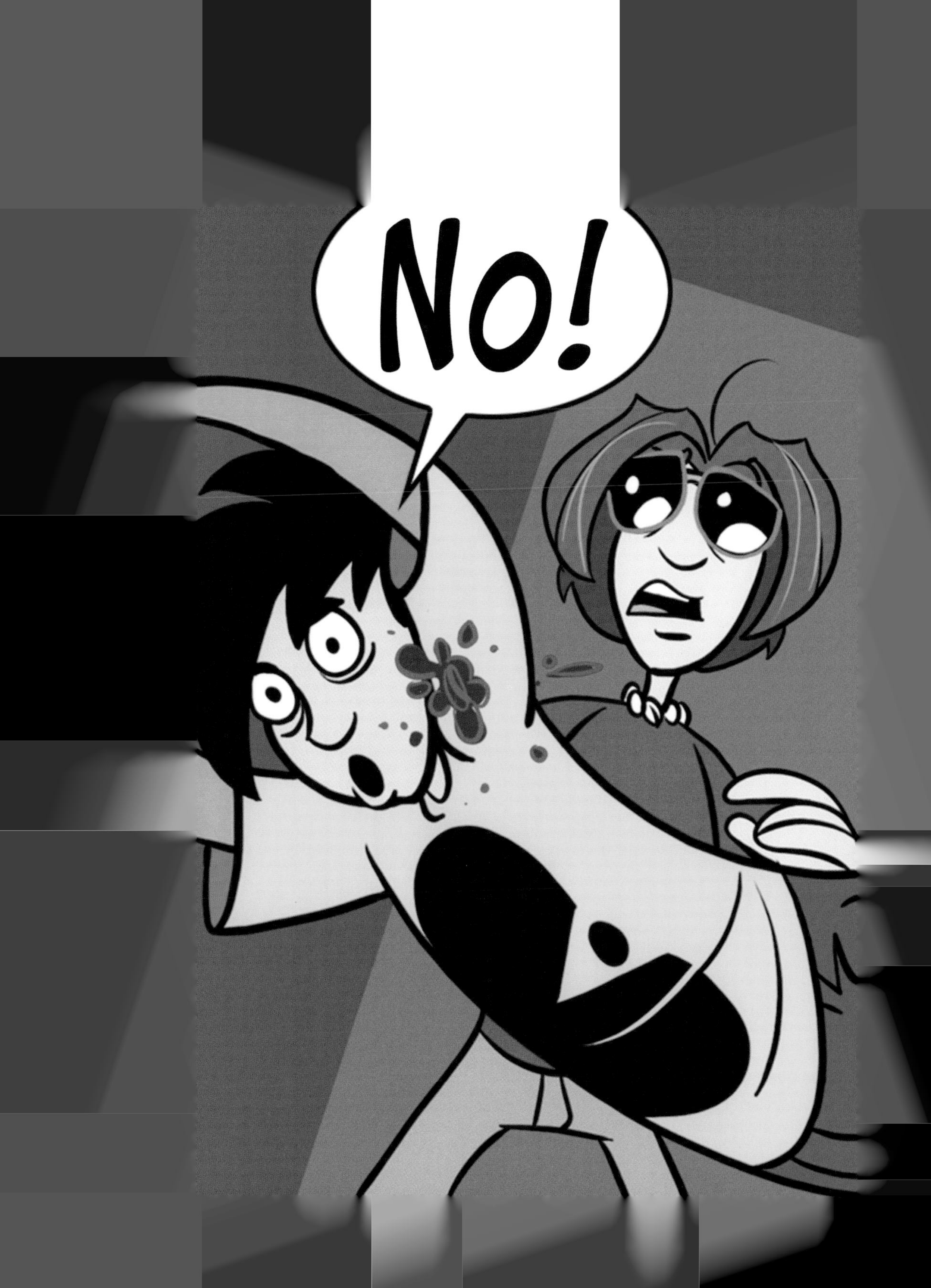
NO!

PEER INTO MY CRYSTAL BALL

August 30, 2006 · This is the strip we drew that year at PAX, and you can see a few additions here that the crowd made. Div and the Hot Dog Fairy in panel three reflect live modifications being made by people at the microphone (or simply people with loud voices). The hand holding the heart, though, is a reference to a specific hand position Gabe draws—check Michael Bay in the comic "Transformers Transfigured" on page 68 to see an example.

AN UNSEEMLY GRIP

September 1, 2006 · This strip is actually about Robert Khoo's feet, not Gabriel's, but it didn't really matter whose feet they were for strip purposes. Robert's toes are crazy long, longer than you would think, longer than is proper for a human toe. His feet look like spiders, like he's just got some spiders down there goin' crazy, and the scuttling, sideways walk he does on those mutant talons constitutes a hellish ballet.

PRINNY PLEASE

September 4, 2006 · I'm nuts about these Prinny things, the weird devil birds that crop up in games from Nippon Ichi Software. I have a wide selection of Prinny memorabilia, including (at one time) a Prinny mask I got at San Diego Comic-Con that made my son practically cry on sight. I found it in the garbage one day when I came home from work, which wasn't a huge surprise. Message received, son. You know? Message received.

ARMS AREN'T EVEN THAT COOL

September 6, 2006 · The "Arms" referenced by the title are those of Enchanted Arms, originally released as the much more elaborate [eM] -eNCHANT arM- in Japan by From Software. It wasn't about to change the world, but we thought the game was better than it was being given credit for. The sins it was being asked to account for were those of JRPGs in general, traits like linearity and hours of tactical combat. Yup, sounds about right.

SQUARE ENIX.

SUPER MARIO BROS. XII
スーパーマリオブラザーズⅩⅡ

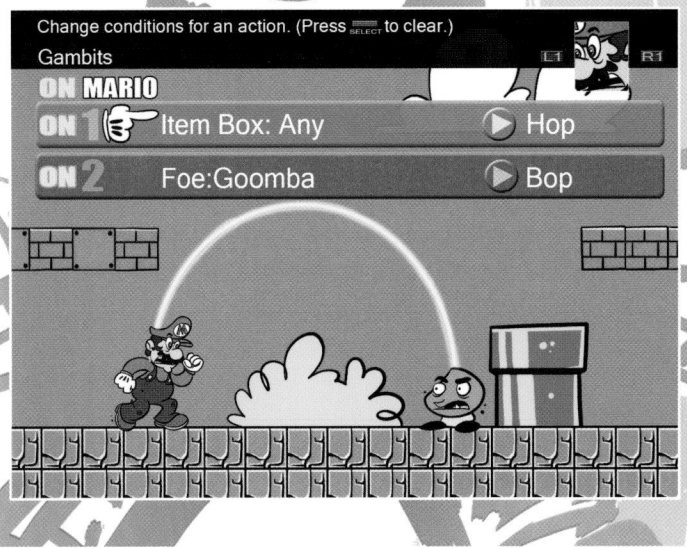

NEW FROM SQUAREENIX

September 8, 2006 · Speaking of JPRGs, we found every frame of pre-release hype for Final Fantasy XII beyond vile. And I don't mean beyond vile to a place that is no longer vile—rather, I mean beyond vile to a place that is even more vile than it was originally. At some point in this continuum, Gabriel underwent a full conversion and shifted into Love Mode. I never came around, ever, which is only noteworthy because that's typically *my* arc.

HORSE D'OEUVRES

September 11, 2006 · Because of the Internet, you can know entirely new types of things. In the Web-less depravity of the before-now, if Willie Nelson were thwarting French horse-eaters on the mad, wild plains of America, this secret war would be entirely unknown to you. You would have suffered in the absence of this specialist knowledge. Now this data—and so much more—is fired directly into your corneas.

A BIRD MISUSED

September 13, 2006 · It may be hard to remember just how elemental the PlayStation Network was when it launched, given that they've spent every year since trying to fashion a competitor to Xbox Live. Even at the time of this writing it lacks features I consider fundamental, features that greater integration with Xfire would have delivered in a slick, cross-platform package.

WIIACTIONS

September 15, 2006 · I'm glad we cataloged this stuff here, because the period since has been an almost unbroken vertical climb of industry-defining success for the hardware. Four years after the Wii saw the retail shelf, both of its primary competitors relaunched their own hardware in an effort to bite some portion of Nintendo's style. It's been incredible to watch.

ASSUME THE WORST

September 18, 2006 · I was getting that flash card for our Podcast Recording Machine, which has lain fallow lo these many months. We had a lot of fun doing podcasts, and people enjoyed listening to them, which is what you're looking for in these situations. We had a hard time keeping to a schedule on them because it was, well, a schedule. Robert's idea to film the stuff that goes on in the office—what we now call PATV—hopefully fills some portion of the void.

IN BREACH OF WARRANTY

September 20, 2006 · Mario Hoops 3 on 3 has, I think, fallen through the cracks of history. It is very cool, though, and not just for hoops, but for a truly startling multiplayer offering I've never heard discussed—Coin Race. Imagine playing deathmatch with denizens from the Marioverse and you'll know exactly what I mean. Who made this crazy thing? Why is it on there? Ask around. *Nobody knows.*

EASTERN DELIGHTS

September 22, 2006 · Whenever I watch Japanese trailers, I'm always very curious what I'm missing. Maybe the voice-over is the same kind of "In a world . . ." stuff we get, maybe it isn't. Mostly I'm wondering about the characters I see, what Japanese clichés they represent, and how they might differ from my native archetypes. Is there something particular about their "tough guy"? Their "battle woman"? Their "sullen teen"?

THE SECRET WEAPON

September 25, 2006 · It's incredibly funny to me that Sony was talking about games like Final Fantasy and Gran Turismo as serious considerations when they launched that machine. The games didn't come out for another four years, a period of time that saw the world around the system shift into something unrecognizable by the standards of the industry. That is to say, it saw the device and its intended audience enter a state of diminished primacy.

STRIPMINING

September 27, 2006 · One of the earlier attempts to co-opt "webcomics," the contours of the Platinum deal weren't bad by "deal" standards—which is to say they're something that a creator who can afford to should probably avoid. It's going to happen at some point for you, believe it: Some Goddamn reptile will creep into your inbox having seen your work somewhere, and he'll bait his hook with whatever he thinks will make your tummy grumble. Please promise me you will be careful.

MYSTERIES OF THE DEEP

September 29, 2006 · Gabe's house is a kind of shrine to Ariel and *The Little Mermaid* in general. I had always assumed these statues and snow globes and busts and figurines and dolls and crabs and compact discs and watches and Christmas ornaments and wallets and key chains and lunch boxes and false tails belonged to his wife, Kara, when maybe he's still wishing for THE ONE THAT GOT AWAY hoooooooooo.

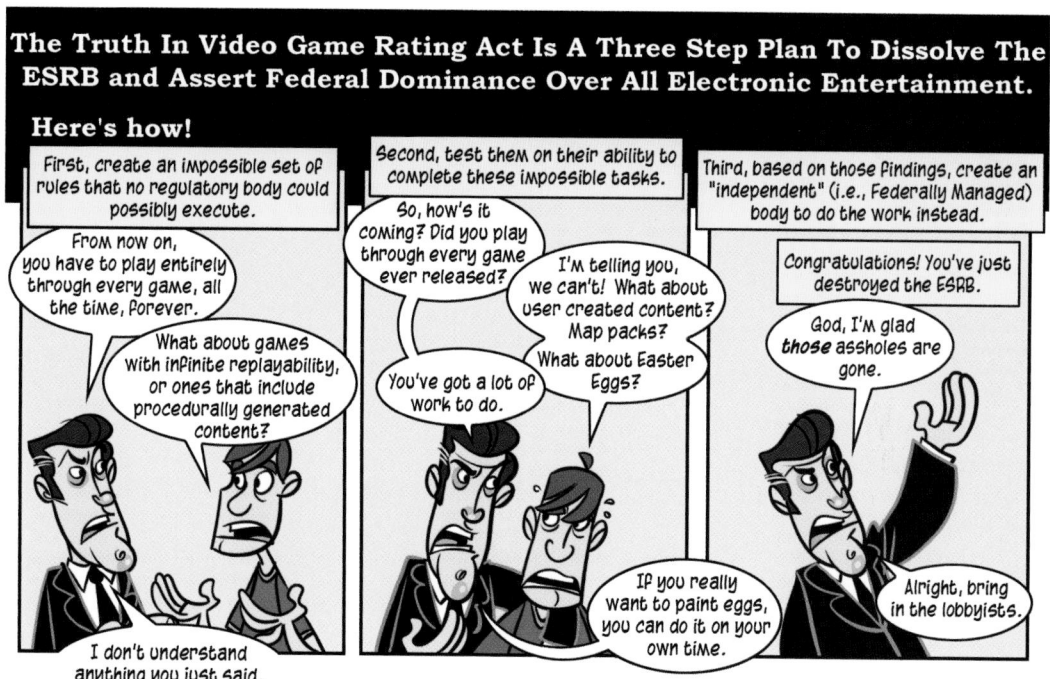

CENSORSHIP MADE EASY

October 2, 2006 · This was all back when "Hot Coffee" and the Oblivion "Nude Patch" were front-page news, and not just at the kind of sites you or I might read. The idea that the Entertainment Software Rating Board needed to play every game through in its entirety (even though the content that everyone found so objectionable would never have been *seen* in the course of normal play) more or less gave the game away. This kind of broad political maneuver died down for a while, but it might be making a comeback.

Knock on wood. Make sure it's actual wood, though, and not just some kind of laminate. There's no luck in *there*.

ZUNE AND VERY ZUNE

October 4, 2006 · The truth is that I actually liked the Zune. It improved considerably over the years, with software updates that brought older devices forward with the platform. When it began to leverage its social music capabilities online, I thought, *Hey!*—but none of that stuff really mattered. Had a radio; didn't matter. Slick new form factor, sharp organic light emitting diode on there; no dice. Eventually, all the iPod I would ever need was built into my phone. Sometimes you can't win for losing.

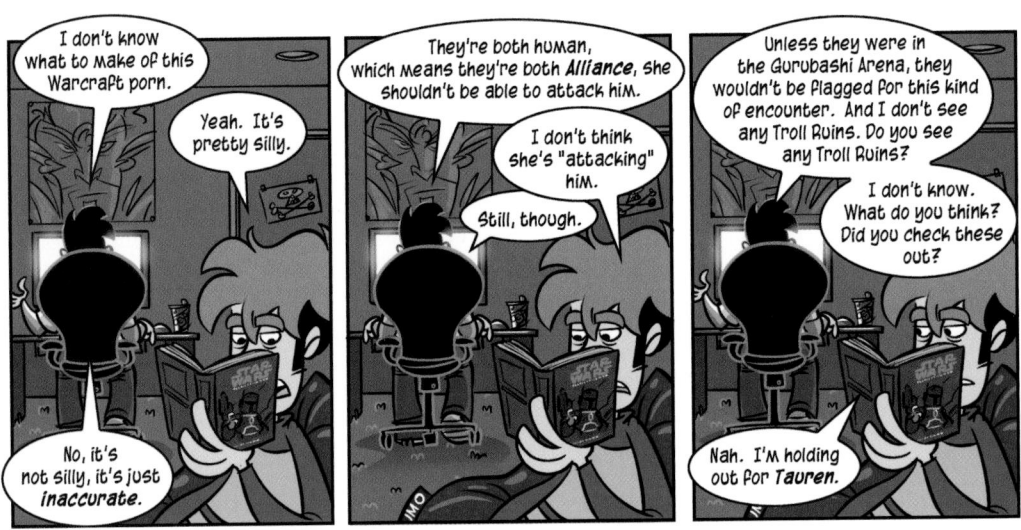

IMPRECISION (AS IT RELATES TO EROTICA)

October 6, 2006 · We were surprised, though perhaps not *very* surprised, to see "World of Whorecraft" emerge on the scene. Apparently Blizzard wasn't impressed with the name, though I have a hard time believing that anyone would confuse the two products; it may be that procreation is a feature they are saving for a future expansion. The name of the project was eventually changed to WhoreLore, presumably to draw attention to its rich narrative.

JOHN GABRIEL, *DENTISTA*

October 9, 2006 · The Winter Solstice Times Holiday in 2006 was especially devastating, clocking in at something like fifteen hundred dollars apiece if we were to investigate everything we had a genuine interest in. We felt confident in the math, because Robert had done it, and folded the data into a somber PowerPoint deck. A PlayStation 3 would have been five to six hundred dollars more than that, which is to say, *yow.*

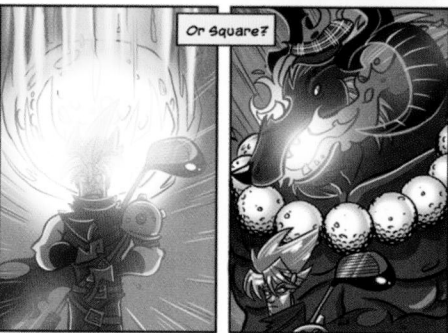

GOLF EVOLVED

October 11, 2006 · I love golf only a sliver of the amount that Gabriel does, but that's already quite a lot. I can't actually play the game, and I don't own any "equipment" for golf outside of a single sky-blue polo shirt. I'll never turn down an offer to go, though. Gabriel and I created an entire RPG universe called Golgolfa on the course once, and it was incredibly elaborate. I don't want to go too deep into it, but you may be certain that balls of various elemental polarities featured prominently.

THE GREEN HARVEST, PART ONE

October 13, 2006 · We set up a charity poker tournament for Child's Play in 2006, and it's something we should do again, because it was a complete blast. I lasted a lot longer than I expected to, all the way to the final table as I recall. Also: Don't forget! Tonkatsu is the Cardboard Tube Samurai's pig. I don't know what it's called when you refer to *your own work* inside your work. And then I'm referring to it again, here in the text! This is clearly some M. C. Escher–type shit.

THE GREEN HARVEST, PART TWO

October 16, 2006 · I really did need to teach him poker, by the way. People need to be taught things they don't know. I'm not saying that this is bad necessarily, but poker just seems so . . . fundamental, like knowing how to play chess (though he might not know that one, either). Perhaps the answer lies in the home; in my own family, we played a lot of games. It was much, much better than talking to one another.

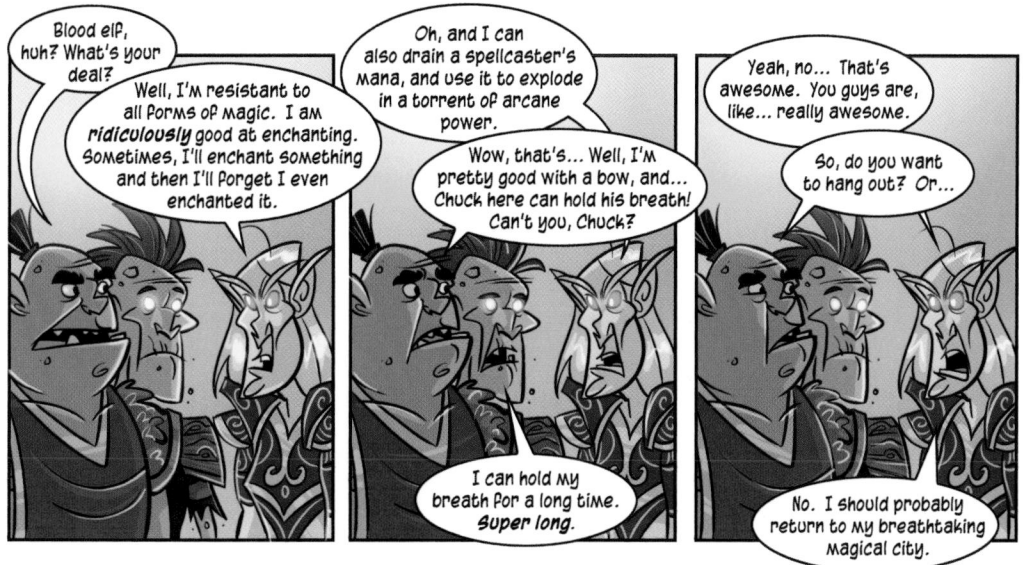

STARK COMPARISONS

October 18, 2006 · I sort of get the lore reasons, but as a matter of raw aesthetics blood elves are weird and everything but they're not warty green brutes or cannibals or undead guys or a minotaur. They never really struck me as capital *H* capital *M Horde Material.* I don't know. They have some kinda crazy eyebrows, I guess. That's about it.

ADVERTISING IN THE FUTURE

October 20, 2006 · Wasn't this supposed to be the thing? It happened every now and then, sure, but in-game advertising was supposed to be the new frontier or something, right? And then it happened a couple of times, and then didn't happen a whole lot after that?

THE UGLIEST MAN ALIVE

October 23, 2006 · Jeezle Chreezle, but you could make some real mutants on that thing. Any of those things, really, the whole genre of face and scalp customizations. One of the most chilling for us personally is still Rainbow Six, which lets you map a picture of your own face onto your model. It really freaked my mom out to see her son gunned down over and over, let me tell you. Not a fan.

MISDIRECTION

October 25, 2006 · We never invested a lot of imagination in what precise shape this Spreader might take, or how its rubberized actuators might manipulate a given region. We felt confident that the grisly *specificity* of this instrument would deliver its dark payload. Also, Sam Fisher really does have that thing on his back all the time for no reason. It really is very strange!

BRITISH SPOKEN HERE

October 27, 2006 · It's exceedingly rare that any shenanigans are required to get something in my global "region," where choice cuts are the norm when it comes to media distribution—but this was the rare case. Creating an account in Wales (as I did) was much more elaborate than I expected; it wanted a lot of specific information that required research. I learned a lot in the process, actually. I may be an honorary Welshman.

NIGHTMARE AT TWENTY-THOUSAND FEET

October 30, 2006 · I never turn my shit off, no way. I feel like such a gangster when I leave my eReader in sleep mode during takeoff and landing. You know what I mean? Like a full-on, apocalyptic gangster in some blasted husk of a modern city. Just straight-up hardcore from head to toe, all totems and trophies from my enemies and a wicked chain coiled like a ready snake.

BA DUM BUM PSH

November 1, 2006 · I never really watched enough *Lost* to be angry at its meandering arcs or its smoke beasts.

ACTS OF CORD

November 3, 2006 · Are there people who like this thing? Or these *things,* as a category? I like the industrial design, and the integration into the hardware, but I never had a Bluetooth headset phase so I never got used to the constant weight of some Uhura-type shit hanging on or coming out of my human ear. I'm not a huge fan of cords—I'm not *pro-cord*—but I never found the tiny, thin cable of the standard headset especially tyrannical.

AGE AIN'T NOTHING BUT A NUMBER

November 6, 2006 · Occasionally we have a genuine fight about something that ends up making its way into the strip as a "joke" when what's really happened is that we've used the comic strip itself as a third-party mediator. He doesn't understand why I would compare today's games with games from ten years ago, and I don't understand why he doesn't understand. Status: unresolved.

HIJINKS ENSUE

November 8, 2006 · The deeper into this year we get, the more clear it is that 2006 set the stage for the last several years. Not just chronologically, though that is certainly true as well. If you want to have a 2007, it helps to have a 2006. It helps *a lot.* But every piece was placed on the board, the opening gambits unfolding in slow motion, and much about their current positions can be seen here. Gears gave the Xbox portfolio—where exclusives are few and far between—some much-needed heft.

MEET MR. HYDE

November 10, 2006 · I still don't know when I'm doing this, and what's more I don't think of myself as a person who does, so it's always surprising to find out how poorly I have behaved in a given instance. It's not just games, it's any contest. But when Kiko missed three attacks in a row in last night's Warmachine game I said "Yay yayi!" in the manner of Ice Cube and then entered a B-boy stance. Maybe that wasn't entirely necessary.

YOU KNOW IT TO BE TRUE

November 13, 2006 · True, true, true. And it has not ceased being true in the intervening period.

READING BETWEEN THE LINES

November 15, 2006 · There's Horse Armor, right, and we've discussed that (see page 32). But that was only one way to approach the idea of downloadable content, and in the primordial fluid that birthed this generation of consoles it got stranger still. There were many offerings then that delivered not what we would think of as "content," but things like skill points or in-game money—things that, just one year previous, would have been the kind of things you'd get from a cheat code.

MAXIMUM MOISTURE

November 17, 2006 · The system got to a good place, eventually, through years of hard work and process of steadily walking back the functionality of the hardware to realize some cost savings. Indeed, things have come so far that it's hard to recall its scandalous initial asking price, rank offerings like Lair, or the fact that the same games often ran better on the competitors' less expensive hardware.

A WORD OF THANKS

November 20, 2006 · These playstyle differences really allowed us to reap human lives, because Rainbow Six: Vegas looks just like a first-person shooter, but it isn't. It had (has, I guess; it's still real) an incredibly smart toggle system for entering cover, which transforms the affair into a third-person action game. Easily, *easily* some of the best time I've spent online.

THE TURKEY TRILOGY, EPISODE ONE

November 22, 2006 · We introduced the idea of Tycho's niece to some success, and also the idea that Tycho and her father don't get along especially well, which was an idea that originally came out of the game we helped make, On the Rain-Slick Precipice of Darkness. In that game, Tycho's brother actually leaves and changes his last name to *Forthwith.* I had sort of forgotten he was in here, and I'd also forgotten how vicious he is. I mean, check out the next strip.

THE TURKEY TRILOGY, EPISODE TWO

November 24, 2006 · I think there's a few interesting bits here, but specifically I like the idea that there's someone to counter Tycho in his own mode. Gabe is a great, implacable foil for Tycho, and their battling energies set the stage for the entire comic. But he offers the *opposite* of Tycho's spin. The difference here is that the man in this strip is actually a better Tycho than Tycho himself.

THE TURKEY TRILOGY, EPISODE THREE

November 27, 2006 · Part of the idea for this story line was generated when Gabriel came to Thanksgiving at my grandma Shirley's house. The woman is a dynamo, a font of limitless energy and culinary power. The poster shown here is real, and may even be the source of that power. It's downstairs in her sewing room, right inside the door, and he is always happy to see her.

LUBRICADO

November 29, 2006 · The winter of 2006 was a serious one, at least by Seattle standards, where any winter whatsoever scratches the veneer of civilization off the entire town. Anyway, Gabriel couldn't escape the hill outside his house, so he constructed this strip according to the old ways. We were trying to imagine this rash of broken televisions in the wake of the Wii launch, and thought different slimes might be to blame. At the end of the day, though, Nintendo must have agreed it was a problem. They changed their strap design, and then they starting making that huge rubber sheath thingy to put on your controllers.

HOOKWORM ADVENTURES

December 1, 2006 · I used to take screenshots of the words I would create in Bookworm Adventures—for real—the same way a person might take shots of their children or a beloved hound. That seems a little wacky, even for me, but I lost them all in a hard drive crash and I miss them terribly. I once used all sixteen tiles on a word, and I still tingle with the remembrance of it.

'TIS THE SEASON (FOR DECEIT)

December 4, 2006 · Oh, look! It's Div. I wonder what he's doing these days.

RAINBOW SUX

December 6, 2006 · They were screwing around with the voice support in this game, changing the way it worked, and not for the best in every case. Before they began messing around with it, it had a proximity voice feature that Gabriel used to taunt our foes. There are other games that have proximity voices, but they don't have the *pace* of Rainbow Six, so something like a conversation isn't really practical. Good God, he had me on the floor with some of this shit.

APPARENTLY QUITE AMUSING

December 8, 2006 · Gabriel can't keep his hands off the Ventrilo name field, loves to enter things in it that aren't names, likes to use it as a venue for communication. Likes to have conversations with it. He also likes to suggest that the computer is saying these things without his active participation, so that he can pretend to be some kind of impartial fucking observer. It's incredible, the whole thing is just fucking incredible.

MORE CAUTIOUS THAN OPTIMISTIC

December 11, 2006 · Whatever happened to this thing, I wonder? A quick glance at FireflyMMO.com (in a post dated September 4, 2008) suggests that "Fox's plans for the development of the previously announced Firefly MMOG have been delayed, but Fox looks forward to continuing its collaboration with Multiverse on this endeavor." I think that basically means something like "fuck you," right?

THE NEXT STEP

December 13, 2006 · I referred to this earlier in the book, a "viral" marketing campaign for the PSP that leveraged "guerrilla marketing" in the form of terrible rap flows and other bullshit (see "They Are Among Us"). Referring to the video, I said in the post that:

> there can be no doubt: the man has been lobotomized. There is no man *left*. In the video, the meat continues to twitch, electrical accidents birthing grotesque jerks in the unknowing beef. It speaks! But it is not language. It is like the wind blowing through a pile of skulls.

DEFINITION THEATER

December 15, 2006 · Some of the imagery of these injured souls was actually hard to look at, and with the rise of the motion controller it may be that we're in for another round. For Kinect, anyway. People like to make fun of the Move controller's plump gland or whatever is going on at the end there—that squishy rubber ball—but I bet you'd rather be hit in the eye by a pliable bulb than a human fist.

SERIOUSLY, THOUGH, FOR REAL

December 18, 2006 · This was the year we stopped buying software from dedicated retailers. We got tired of being treated like weirdos for going into a game store and trying to buy a game there. I wasn't going into this fucking place trying to buy a hog or some shit. The thing that really made us turn the corner was learning we could just go around the corner to Best Buy or Target or any other place and pick it up without the fucking interrogation.

AND HERE'S GABE WITH THE WEATHER

December 20, 2006 · This one is from 2006? I always liked it: It has a torment factor, which always adds several points. We wanted to touch on it, though, to mark the feature somewhere on the site, just because it seemed so out of the ordinary. Again: This was long before we had any idea that "ordinary" was about to undergo several profound seismic shocks.

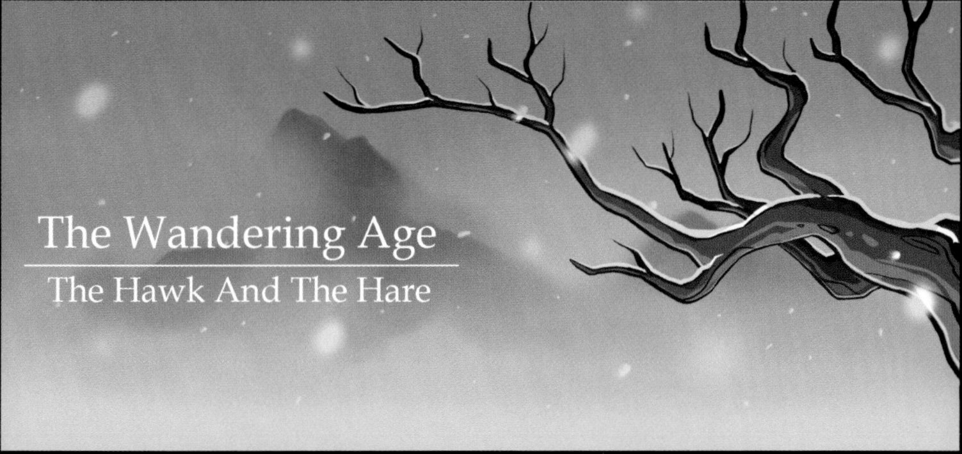
The Wandering Age
The Hawk And The Hare

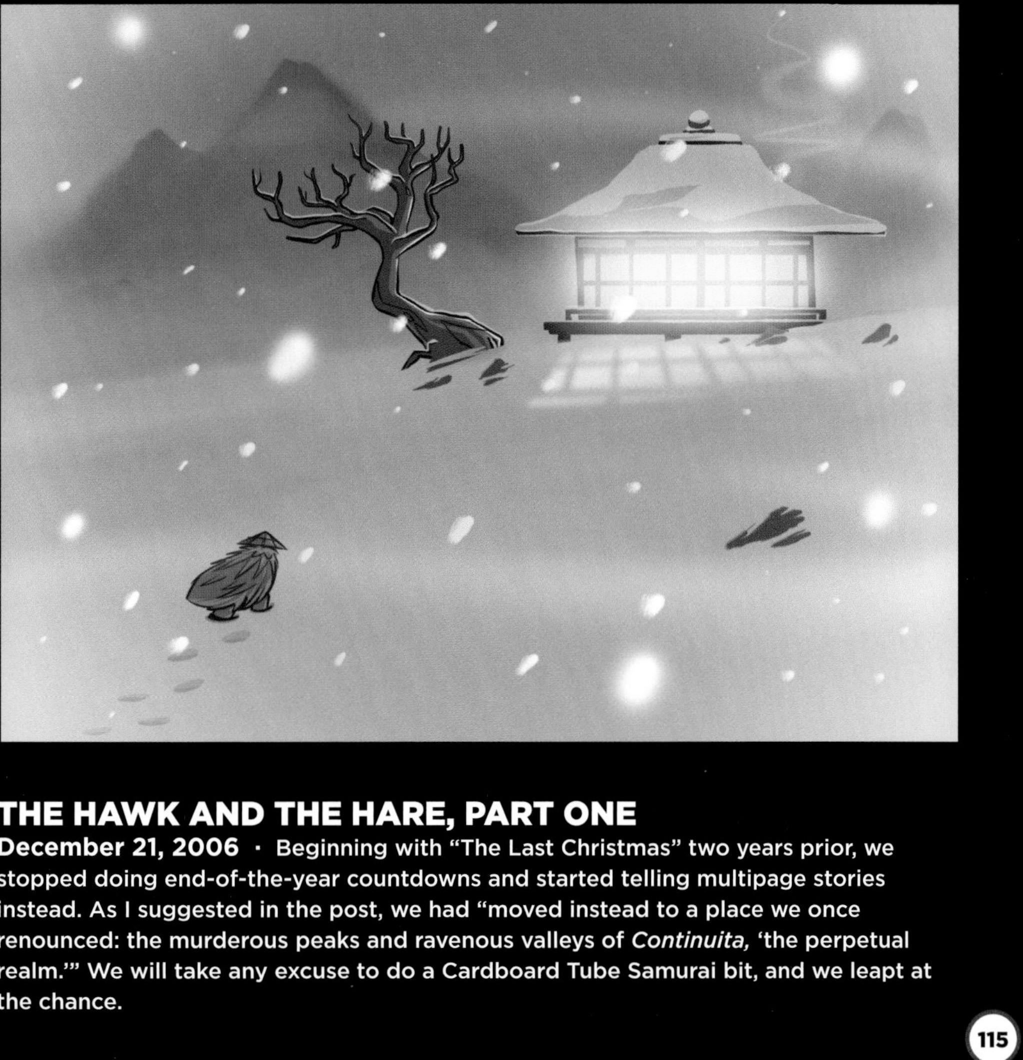

THE HAWK AND THE HARE, PART ONE

December 21, 2006 · Beginning with "The Last Christmas" two years prior, we stopped doing end-of-the-year countdowns and started telling multipage stories instead. As I suggested in the post, we had "moved instead to a place we once renounced: the murderous peaks and ravenous valleys of *Continuita,* 'the perpetual realm.'" We will take any excuse to do a Cardboard Tube Samurai bit, and we leapt at the chance.

THE HAWK AND THE HARE, PART TWO

December 25, 2006 · During the presentation of this series, Gabriel put together a selection of the art and commentary associated with previous Cardboard Tube Samurai adventures. From his post:

These comics introduced a way of telling the CTS stories that we have continued to this da It's the idea of showing the moments directly preceding a fight or immediately after rather than the fight itself. It's an old storytelling device and one that we are absolutely fucking hooked on. Nearly every CTS strip since has incorporated this concept.

THE HAWK AND THE HARE, PART THREE

December 27, 2006 · Looking over at the site, I'm starting to think that you should go over there and take a little bit to read his posts. There's lots of close-ups on panels and the ideas behind them, as well as full pages from the start of a comic called *Purity* that we were doing for Club PA, back when we were still supporting the site with donations. I almost pasted a link right here into the text, but then I remembered that books don't work that way.

THE HAWK AND THE HARE, PART FOUR

December 29, 2006 · We always used to apologize, consciously or unconsciously, whenever we would take over the site for some flight of fancy like this. No doubt this sense that we were acting without your authorization led us to the new system: the one where we place single-page "pitches" for you to vote on, and then move as you have directed. We've had a lot of fun with that so far, and it's a solid new tradition we'll hang on to for a while.

· · ·

Well, that's it for this part of the book. I hope you've enjoyed 2006 as much as I have enjoyed recounting it for you.

L. H. FRANZIBALD'S
Song of the Sorcelator
BY L. H. FRANZIBALD

I am L. H. Franzibald.

Well, no. I just thought it would be funny to have that sentence after the logo. I am the same person who wrote everything else in this book, that is to say, some admixture of Tycho Brahe and Jerry Holkins. I wrote much of the official *Sorcelator* material, named its despicable author and so forth, but unlike most of what I write—stuff I generally revile and want desperately to edit immediately after it's published—*The Song of the Sorcelator* represents something I can actually *enjoy* right on the face of it.

It has a similar arc to *Epic Legends of the Hierarchs: The Elemenstor Saga,* which was featured prominently in the last book. Similar but different, in that all this *Sorcelator* business is a parody of something that was *already a parody.* Somehow, and I don't entirely understand the process, this "double parodization" has inverted the flow (of . . . stuff) and resulted in a weird phenomenon that is even more fun than the original thing.

We wanted to reprint (and honor) the community contributions to the setting, which we were constantly inspired by, but we also wanted to put together some original strips for the book. For the new stuff, we wondered how the villainous Franzibald would reimagine his seminal work—or even a later book, such as *Lord of the God-Kings* or his YA, kid-lit play *Wanditos.* We wondered, and then we considered. And after considering, we thought.

We didn't have to think long.

THE SONG OF THE SORCELATOR

A unique combination of fantasy with cyberpunk, post-apocalyptic, and to some extent science fiction and erotic novels, L. H. Franzibald's *The Song of the Sorcelator* has gathered a large force of dedicated readers. It has also garnered its share of equally dedicated detractors.

Following the exploits of the Sorcelator Grimm Shado, *The Song of the Sorcelator* has been described as a "completely ripped work of fantasy, the likes of which the world has never seen" by author L. H. Franzibald. Conversely, Tycho Brahe, author of the epic *Elemenstor Saga,* has labeled the *Sorcelator* novels a "perversion" of the fantasy genre and has accused Franzibald of plagiarism on multiple occasions as well as multiple message boards. He has also posted tweets to this effect, dire tweets of flame and consequence.

To date, the series has four tomes, which constitute a tale of unrivaled badassness that Franzibald has referred to as a "Quartazion." At least one more book is expected.

Tome 1—*The Song of the Sorcelator,* colloquially called *Overturn*

Tome 2—*Night After Dark*

Tome 3—*Eye for an Eye, Wand for a Wand*

Tome 4—*Desert Funeral*

Tome 5—*The Vampire-Pimps and the Zombie-Eyes of Scarlott* (announced, release date unknown)

GRIMM SHADO

Gruff, manly (and dangerous) hero of the brilliant L. H. Franzibald's seminal work *The Song of the Sorcelator,* Grimm Shado is a man on a mission. He is a Sorcelator (really a Xorcelator) of Fieriness and Bedarkening—two of the Elementals (of which there are seven) present in Franzibald's inspired fantasy series—and is separate from the other Sorcelators in that he can manipulate two Elementals at once. This concept, like everything else in the *Sorcelator* books, combines compelling imagery with off-the-cuff cool, drawing the reader in and promoting visceral excitement.

Grimm's quest in life is twofold. Primarily, he searches the post-apocalyptic deserts of his world (Fehtahn) relentlessly for the details of his true parentage, living as a nomadic "Spellbiker." Secondarily, he seeks to darkly and handsomely (and dangerously) score with totally bitchin' hot Cyberpunk Wasteland Chicks.

Throughout the Sorcelator Saga, Grimm fights manifold foes, most of them completely fresh and original—often made even more awesome by their deadly bionic

parts. The Cybercthonicswinemen or the Robo-Chair Brigade are perfect examples of this. Additionally there are several recurring groups of villains who hold numerous dark secrets from Grimm's darkly enshadowed past—most notably, the Pirate Assassins and their Metal Friends, or his archnemesis General Grabflank.

In *Return of the Witchaloks II,* it is revealed that Grimm Shado is the asexually conceived offspring of a Witchalok. Whether he is truly a hermaphroditic androgynite has not, as of yet, been revealed.

Equipment

Grimm Shado's primary weapons, when he is not using his considerable robo-kung-fu prowess to manually pummel his enemies, are his twin cybermagical Wands, Hurt

and Burn. Almost everyone, even the most jaded of fantasy fans, tends to agree that Hurt and Burn are "pretty awesome." Quotes from high-ranking members of the *Song* community, and other communities (even those stupid ELotH:TES *Smellemenstors* know that Hurt and Burn rock!) include "Two wands? That's actually pretty bitchin' man," and "Jesus, think of all the stuff you could do with *two wands.*"

In addition to his twin wands, Grimm possesses cyber-enhanced *triple wand claws.* Like cyberpunk-inspired retractable "spurs" (the best-known example being Wolverine's triple spurs or "claws" in Marvel comic books), these *wand claws* emerge from the back of Grimm's hands; each acts both as a conventional spur (for cutting) and as a wand (bringing the total number of wands Grimm regularly uses to eight).

Grimm also wears an Extreme Leather Coat, and in Tome 2 briefly was in possession of a Sweet Jetpack.

Excerpts

Grimm woke from a deep and dreamless sleep. Perhaps not quite dreamless. Still rolling around the back of his mind it was there. When he tried to focus on it, inevitably it would slip away like radiation through a barred window. It was the song. The haunting melody that sometimes came far enough into his consciousness that he could almost hum it, but then it would again submerge, tauntingly. What was this half-remembered memory that dogged his mind just after waking or just before drifting off to sleep?

—*The Song of the Sorcelator,* page 62

"I am Grimm Shado," said Grimm Shado, his triple wand claws extending. "And I am here to take it to the limit."

—*The Song of the Sorcelator,* page 179

Trivia and Extrania

In each Tome, Grimm encounters one character who is a doppelgänger, clone, half brother, alternate dimension mirror image, or other such copy or variation of himself. At times these characters become allies; others become deadly foes.

An example of this is Slimm Shado from Tome 2 and the recently revealed Tome 5 villain Shrimm Grado.

THE WITCHALOK

A Witchalok is a magical practitioner of Arcanium magic. All Witchaloks are hermaphroditic androgynites, capable of asexual reproduction.

Witchaloks each carry a unique Witchalok Blade that is cybermagically enchanted, and it grants them a unique power or ability.

Witchaloks have appeared in the graphic novel *Blade of the Witchalok*. They also played a prominent role in the film *Return of the Witchaloks II,* as well as appearing in Tome 4.

Grimm Shado may be the child of a Witchalok, which might explain "his" extensive powers.

Maybe.

The Witchalok

"Witchaloks? I don't know anything about any Witchaloks."

Witchaloks are the heirs of a billion-year heritage of baleful sorcery—sorcery substantially more baleful than that of their magical contemporaries. Necromancers are, by Witchalok standards, insufficiently baleful. Defilers entertain children at Witchalok birthday parties. Liches are commonly used as a punch line in Witchalok stand-up routines. Tiamat is almost bad enough—*almost*, but not quite.

Witchalok Class Features

Witchaloks have the following class features.

Nut Allergy

Witchaloks are deathly allergic to nuts and nut by-products, such as nut pastes, oils, and other residues. They must always read labels very carefully.

Polaritude

As a Witchalok, the rigors of your mystical trainery have uncorked heretofore-unknown badass techniques. You are a twisting vortex that vomits necrotic energy, even if you were out super late last night and you just woke up. Choose one of the following options.

WITCHALOK OVERVIEW

Characteristics: Your powers are a heady blend of living bones, reincarnated owls, malign scents, and other things. When you enter the ring, foes often have no idea what's going to happen next, let alone what is happening at this moment—and that's just how you like it. You might compliment them on their capes, which is weird. Then you'll all sing with a marmot who was never actually real. A short time later, they will be dead.

Religion: All Witchaloks revere the Witchalok King to the exclusion of all other powers. Little is known about the Witchalok King, who is known only as King Witchalok. Reports that he either "lays eggs" or is somehow part fish are largely considered apocryphal.

Races: Banished over one million years ago, Witchaloks are true denizens of the Shadowdark. In this terrible span of time, the unknowable energies twisted by these fearsome sorcelators shaped them into an entirely new race called witchaloks, with a small w, which is a little confusing. The end result is that witchaloks make excellent Witchaloks.

CLASS TRAITS

Role: Controller. Leveraging a suite of truly badical eldritch techniques, you char, scourge, and frappe those foolish enough to draw your ire. Depending on your choice of class features and powers, you lean toward being either sweet or totally awesome.

Power Source: Arcane. You are a nonstop torrent of excruciation for would-be interlopers. Witchaloks have a saying: "Those who mess with the Black Bull of Gael'Thoth shall be pierced by their darkhorns."

Key Abilities: Charisma, Dexterity, Constitution

Armor Proficiencies: Cloth, leather

Weapon Proficiencies: Witchalok Blades

Implements: Witchalok Blades (see below)

Bonus to Defense: +1 Fortitude, +1 Reflex, +1 Will

Hit Points at 1st Level: 9 + Constitution score

Hit Points per Level Gained: 5¾

Healing Surges per Day: 6 + Constitution modifier

Trained Skills: Religion. From the class skills list below, choose three more trained skills at 1st level.

Class Skills: Arcana (Int), Diplomacy (Cha), Acrobatics (Dex), History (Int), Insight (Wis), Intimidate (Cha), Streetwise (Cha)

Class Features: Nut Allergy, Polaritude, Witcholese, Hermaphoditic Androgynites, Ritual Casting

Sweet

Whether surfing on an avalanche or jumping off a motorcycle onto the back of a giant bat, there is something about the way you do what you do that makes people say, "Whoa!" When using any of your Witchalok powers, choose one target you have line of sight to. That target is totally blown away.

Awesome

Some Witchaloks are so awesome that people can't even believe it. When people see you get out of a Lamborghini, platinum spinners whirling, ornate robes crisp and pressed, they wonder if they still have time to switch classes. Whenever a target would be pushed by one of your Witchalok powers, that target also wants to hang out sometime maybe, if you aren't too busy.

Witcholese

All Witchaloks can speak unaccented Witcholese.

Hermaphoditic Androgynites

All Witchaloks are considered male and female for purposes of effects related to gender.

Ritual Casting

Witchaloks gain Ritual Casting as a bonus feat.

Implements

Witchaloks rely exclusively on Witchalok Blades to focus their brutal, otherworldly will. Thrumming with malevolent purpose, these blades allow full access to the infinite folds of the Witchweave. Unfortunately, the secrets of their creation are lost to time. Only one pair of Witchalok Blades exists, and all Witchaloks must share them.

Witchalok Powers

Your Witchalok powers are called sorcelations, and you do them mostly by leering a lot and making grim oaths.

Level 1 At-Will Sorcelations

Death Laser   Witchalok Attack 1

As lasers go, this one is pretty good.

At-Will ✦ Arcane, Implement
Standard Action   **Ranged** 10
Target: One creature
Attack: Charisma vs. Reflex
Hit: Target is pushed 2 squares and dies until the end of your next turn.
Level 21: *Aftereffect:* The target dies twice.

Throw Witchalok Blade   Witchalok Attack 1

You throw your Witchalok Blade.

At-Will ✦ Arcane, Implement
Standard Action   **Ranged** 5
Target: One creature
Attack: Dexterity vs. AC
Hit: 1d4 + Dexterity modifier damage. The Witchalok Blade does not return to the user; it must be retrieved from the target's square.
Level 21: Both blades can be thrown. Damage does not increase.

On the Bit
Witchalok Attack 1

Using two fingers, you point at your own eyes, then at your opponent's.

At-Will ✦ Arcane, Implement
Standard Action   **Ranged** 10
Target: One creature
Attack: Charisma vs. Will
Hit: 1d6 + Charisma modifier damage, and the target is placed on the bit.
Level 21: The target apologizes without really knowing why.

LEVEL 1 ENCOUNTER SORCELATIONS

Howl from the Deepest Dark
Witchalok Attack 1

From the rageflames of the Eternal Infernal, you summon a caustic wail.

Encounter ✦ Arcane, Implement
Standard Action   **Close burst** 5
Target: Each creature in burst
Attack: Charisma vs. Fortitude
Hit: Target leaves the area of effect.

Big Skull
Witchalok Attack 1

This skull is really big, and flies all around.

Encounter ✦ Arcane, Skull
Standard Action   **Area burst** 20
Target: One creature in burst
Attack: Charisma vs. Will
Hit: Targets scream and wave their arms wildly. On a critical hit, targets are inconvenienced.

LEVEL 1 DAILY SORCELATIONS

Slow, Dramatic Clapping
Witchalok Attack 1

Secure in your ultimate victory, you take a moment to ironically applaud your foes.

Daily ✦ Arcane
Immediate Reaction   **Close burst** 3
Trigger: An opponent discovers the extent of your evil plot
Target: The fools who stumbled into your lair
Attack: Charisma vs. Will
Hit: 1d12 + Charisma modifier thunder damage.
Effect: Targets are pushed 2 squares.

Make Wolfoids
Witchalok Attack 1

People are okay with the wolf part. It's that oid bit at the end that makes them nervous.

Daily ✦ Arcane, Implement
Standard Action   **Close burst** 3
Effect: You create a wolfoid, and place it in the area of effect. Targets who begin their turn adjacent to a wolfoid are creeped out.

Reveal Parentage
Witchalok Attack 1

With a cruel smile, you leave no doubt: Your opponent is three-quarters witchalok, on his or her mother's side.

Daily ✦ Arcane
Standard Action   **Close burst** 20
Target: One creature in burst
Attack: Charisma vs. Fortitude
Hit: 2d10 + Charisma modifier psychic damage, and ongoing 5 psychic damage (save ends).

LEVEL 2 UTILITY SORCELATIONS

Which Witchalok?
Witchalok Utility 2

In a flash, your self-satisfied smirk becomes three.

At-Will ✦ Arcane, Implement
Minor Action
Effect: Create two duplicates of yourself, and place them in adjacent squares. Each duplicate is a real person with his or her own hopes and dreams. These duplicates die at the start of your next turn.

Turn into a Dinosaur
Witchalok Utility 2

With a yowl of ineffable primality, you transform into a Tyrannosaurus rex.

At-Will ✦ Arcane, Polymorph
Minor Action (Special)
Effect: You shed your already awesome body for one that is even more awesome—that of a huge dinosaur. While in this form, you cannot utilize any Witchalok powers or abilities. You cannot deal damage, even by accident. You can resume your original form as a free action.

Level 3 Encounter Sorcelations

Unburning Coldfire
Witchalok Attack 3

Black flames chill your foe with a dark heat.

Encounter ✦ Arcane, Implement, Fire, Cold
Standard Action   **Ranged** 10
Target: One creature
Attack: Charisma vs. Fortitude
Hit: 2d12 + 1d4 - 1d6 + Charisma modifier burnfrost damage.

Daggerblade of
One Hundred Million Weeping Sorrows
Witchalok Attack 3

Witchalok Miserites knew only too well the secrets of crushing melancholy.

Encounter ✦ Arcane, Implement, Necrotic
Standard Action   **Ranged** 5
Target: One creature
Attack: Dexterity vs. Will
Hit: 3d8 + Charisma modifier necrotic damage, and the target is sad (save ends).

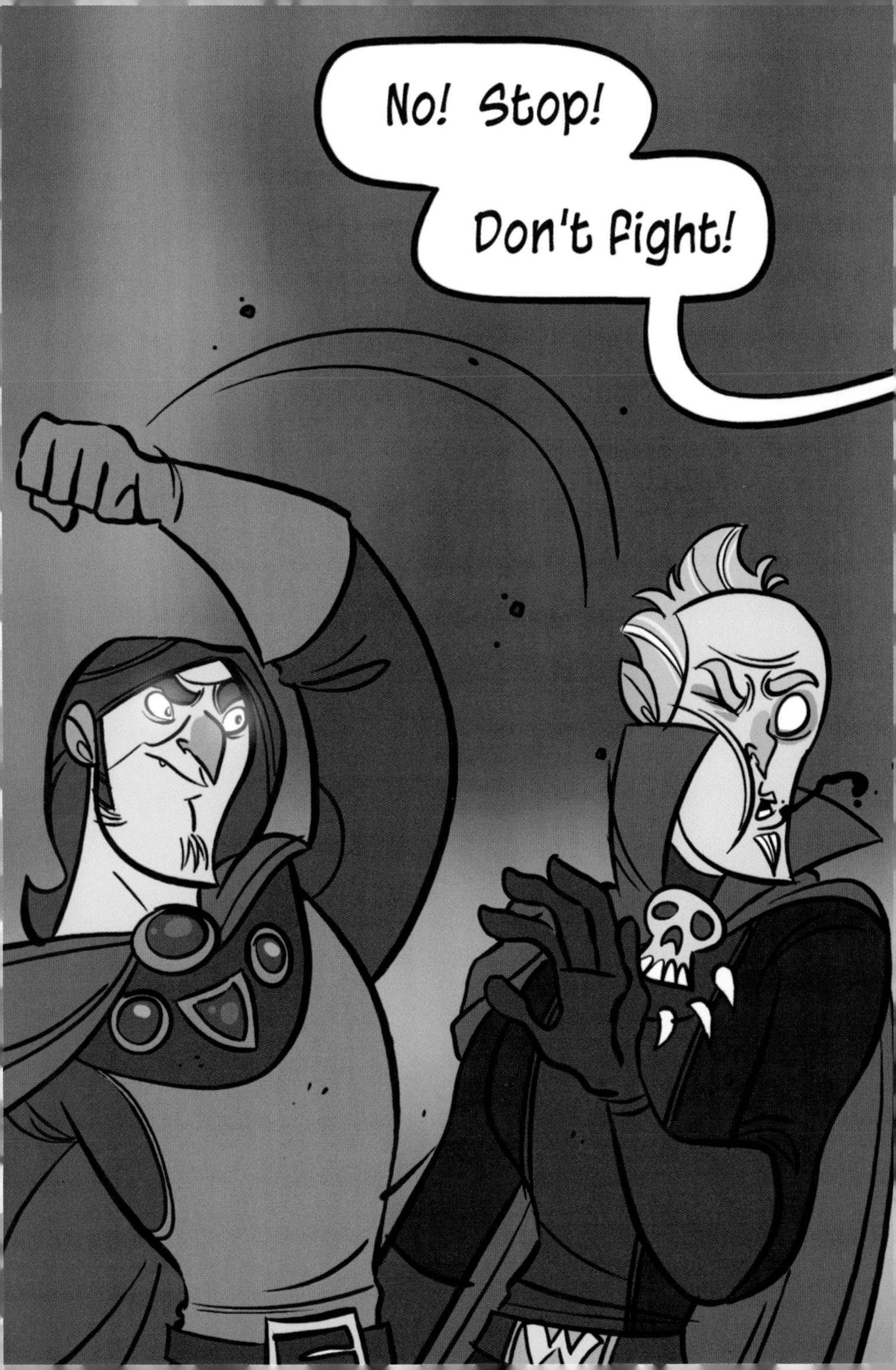
No! Stop!
Don't fight!

THE MOST POPULAR WEBCOMIC
FOR GAMERS, BY GAMERS
GET YOUR GEEK ON!
PENNY ARCADE
1
Jerry Holkins & Mike Krahulik
ATTACK OF THE BACON ROBOT
PENNY ARCADE
2
Jerry Holkins & Mike Krahulik
Epic Legends of the MAGIC SWORD KINGS
3
Jerry Holkins & Mike Krahulik
THE WARSUN PROPHECIES
Birds ARE Weird
PENNY ARCADE
4
PENNY ARCADE
THE CASE OF THE MUMMY'S GOLD
PENNY ARCADE
5
Jerry Holkins & Mike Krahulik
NOW IN PRINT!
AVAILABLE AT YOUR LOCAL COMICS SHOP OR BOOKSTORE
To find a comics shop in your area, call 1-888-266-4226
For more information or to order direct visit DarkHorse.com or call 1-800-862-0052
DARK HORSE BOOKS
Penny Arcade™ © 2011 Jerry Holkins and Mike Krahulik. Dark Horse Books® and the Dark Horse logo are registered trademarks of Dark Horse Comics, Inc.

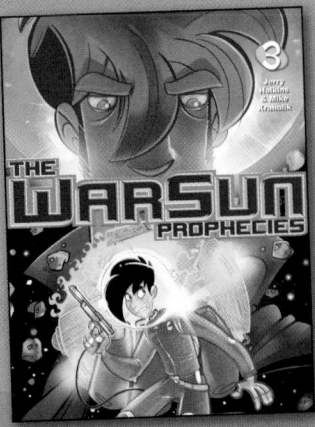

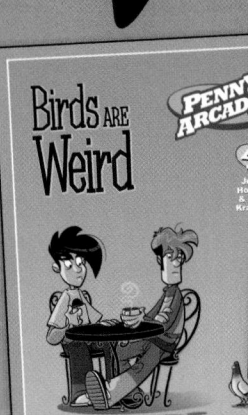

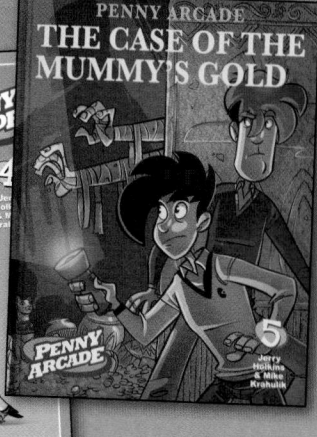